Louis Althusser

transitions
General Editor: Julian Wolfreys

Published titles
BATAILLE Fred Botting and Scott Wilson
NEW HISTORICISM AND CULTURAL MATERIALISM John Brannigan
POSTMODERN NARRATIVE THEORY Mark Currie
FORMALIST CRITICISM AND READER-RESPONSE THEORY Todd F. Davis and Kenneth Womack
QUEER THEORIES Donald E. Hall
MARXIST LITERARY AND CULTURAL THEORIES Moyra Haslett
LOUIS ALTHUSSER Warren Montag
JACQUES LACAN Jean-Michel Rabaté
LITERARY FEMINISMS Ruth Robbins
DECONSTRUCTION•DERRIDA Julian Wolfreys

ORWELL TO THE PRESENT: LITERATURE IN ENGLAND, 1945–2000 John Brannigan
FROM CHAUCER TO SHAKESPEARE, 1337–1580 SunHee Kim Gertz
BURKE TO BYRON, BARBAULD TO BAILLIE, 1790–1830 Jane Stabler
FROM MILTON TO POPE, 1650–1720 Kay Gilliland Stevenson
SIDNEY TO MILTON, 1580–1660 Marion Wynne-Davies

Forthcoming titles
TERRY EAGLETON David Alderson
JULIA KRISTEVA AND LITERARY THEORY Megan Becker-Leckrone
NATIONAL IDENTITY John Brannigan
HÉLÈNE CIXOUS: WRITING AND SEXUAL DIFFERENCE Abigail Bray
HOMI BHABHA Eleanor Byrne
GENDER Claire Colebrook
IDEOLOGY James Decker
POSTMODERNISM•POSTMODERNITY Martin McQuillan
ROLAND BARTHES Martin McQuillan
RACE Brian G. Niro
MODERNITY David Punter
PSYCHOANALYSIS AND LITERATURE Nicholas Rand
SUBJECTIVITY Ruth Robbins
POSTCOLONIAL THEORY Malini Johan Schueller
TRANSGRESSION Julian Wolfreys

IMAGE TO APOCALYPSE, 1910–1945 Jane Goldman
POPE TO BURNEY, 1714–1779 Moyra Haslett
PATER TO FORSTER, 1873–1924 Ruth Robbins
DICKENS TO HARDY, 1837–1884 Julian Wolfreys

---

transitions Series
Series Standing Order
ISBN 0–333–73684–6
(*outside North America only*)

You can receive future titles in this series as they are published by placing a standing order. Please contact your bookseller or, in case of difficulty, write to us at the address below with your name and address, the title of the series and the ISBN quoted above.

Customer Services Department, Macmillan Distribution Ltd
Houndmills, Basingstoke, Hampshire RG21 6XS, England

---

transitions

Louis Althusser

Warren Montag

palgrave
macmillan

First published 2003 by
PALGRAVE MACMILLAN
Houndmills, Basingstoke, Hampshire RG21 6XS and
175 Fifth Avenue, New York, N.Y. 10010
Companies and representatives throughout the world

PALGRAVE MACMILLAN is the global academic imprint of the Palgrave Macmillan division of St. Martin's Press, LLC and of Palgrave Macmillan Ltd. Macmillan® is a registered trademark in the United States, United Kingdom and other countries. Palgrave is a registered trademark in the European Union and other countries.

ISBN 0–333–91898–3 hardback
ISBN 0–333–91899–1 paperback

This book is printed on paper suitable for recycling and made from fully managed and sustained forest sources.

A catalogue record for this book is available from the British Library.

Library of Congress Cataloging-in-Publication Data
Montag, Warren
Louis Althusser / Warren Montag.
p. cm. – (Transitions)
Includes bibliographical references and index.
ISBN 0-333–91898–3 (cloth)
1. Althusser, Louis–Contributions in criticism. 2. Criticism.
I. Title. II. Series.

PN81 .M59 2002
801'.95'092–dc21 2002028678

10 9 8 7 6 5 4 3 2 1
12 11 10 09 08 07 06 05 04 03

Printed in China

Para Dolores, Elisa y Jacobo

אין אנדענק פון יעקב און רבקה מאנטאג

Contents

General Editor's Preface

> Transitions: *transition*—, n. of action. 1. A passing or passage from one condition, action or (rarely) place, to another. 2. Passage in thought, speech, or writing, from one subject to another. 3. **a**. The passing from one note to another. **b**. The passing from one key to another, modulation. 4. The passage from an earlier to a later stage of development or formation ... change from an earlier style to a later; a style of intermediate or mixed character ... the historical passage of language from one well-defined stage to another.

The aim of *Transitions* is to explore passages, movements and the development of significant voices in critical thought, as these voices determine and are mediated by acts of literary and cultural interpretation. This series also seeks to examine the possibilities for reading, analysis and other critical engagements which the very idea of transition – such as the transition effected by the reception of a thinker's *oeuvre* and the heritage entailed – makes possible. The writers in this series unfold the movements and modulations of critical thinking over the last generation, from the first emergences of what is now recognized as literary theory. They examine as well how the transitional nature of theoretical and critical thinking is still very much in operation, guaranteed by the hybridity and heterogeneity of the field of literary studies. The authors in the series share the common understanding that, now more than ever, critical thought is both in a state of transition and can best be defined by developing for the student reader an understanding of this protean quality. As this *tranche* of the series, dealing with particular critical voices, addresses, it is of great significance, if not urgency, that the texts of particular figures be reconsidered anew.

This series desires, then, to enable the reader to transform her/his own reading and writing transactions by comprehending past developments as well as the internal transitions worked through by particular literary and cultural critics, analysts, and philosophers. Each book in the series offers a guide to the poetics and politics of such thinkers, as well as interpretative paradigms, schools, bodies of thought, historical and cultural periods, and the genealogy of particular concepts, while transforming these, if not into tools or methodologies, then into conduits for directing and channelling thought. As well as transforming the critical past by interpreting it from the perspective of the present day, each study enacts transitional readings of critical voices and well-known literary texts, which are themselves conceivable as having been transitional and influential at the moments of their first appearance. The readings offered in these books seek, through close critical reading and theoretical engagement, to demonstrate certain possibilities in critical thinking to the student reader.

It is hoped that the student will find this series liberating because rigid methodologies are not being put into place. As all the dictionary definitions of the idea of transition above suggest, what is important is the action, the passage: of thought, of analysis, of critical response, such as are to be found, for example, in the texts of critics whose work has irrevocably transformed the critical landscape. Rather than seeking to help you locate yourself in relation to any particular school or discipline, this series aims to put you into action, as readers and writers, travellers between positions, where the movement between poles comes to be seen as of more importance than the locations themselves.

Julian Wolfreys

Acknowledgments

I wish to thank Julian Wolfreys for giving me the opportunity to write this book and for his support and encouragement. I am grateful to the following people for their help and advice: Étienne Balibar, Dan Fineman, Geoff Goshgarian, Pierre Macherey, Herb Patterson, Erin Post, Ted Stolze and John Swift, among many others. The late Michael Sprinker discussed many of the issues explored in this book with me over the years; he saw the significance of Althusser's pieces on theater and art long before I did. I also want to thank my research assistants: Viviana Macmanus, Susan Jonaitis, Jessica Perry, Cynthia Marugg and Jenny Lau.

I would also like to thank Verso for allowing me to include Althusser's essay "On Brecht and Marx" and the translator, Max Statkiewicz, for his support.

The author and publisher would like to thank the following for permission to reproduce copyright material:

Verso, for the extracts from Louis Althusser's *Reading Capital* and *For Marx* (both published in London), and *Essays in Self-Criticism* (Norfolk).

Every effort has been made to trace the copyright-holders, but if any have been inadvertently overlooked, the publisher will be pleased to make the necessary arrangement at the first opportunity.

Introduction

At the time of his death in 1990, one might have legitimately questioned the need for a book on Althusser and literary theory. At that moment, it appeared that Althusser's influence on cultural and literary studies had waned considerably; the terms and concepts taken from or associated with his works and those of his closest associates, such as Pierre Macherey and Étienne Balibar,[1] were seen with declining frequency; when they did appear they gave the work in which they were cited a dated air. In part, of course, this might be attributed to the fact that Althusser worked within a Marxist problematic, a problematic which by all accounts had been superseded both in practice and in theory. In literary studies, the field once occupied by Marxism had yielded to apparently rival theories, such as the New Historicism, whose very origins lay in a critique of Marxism by a number of its leading practitioners (Gallagher 1989). But perhaps even more damningly, the most well-known Marxist critics sought at this time to distance themselves from Althusser and "Althusserianism." Terry Eagleton, whose work was once routinely cited in tandem with Althusser's, now openly argued that the Althusserian legacy was, on balance, rather more negative than positive and felt compelled to distance himself from Althusser and all things French. At the same time, Frederic Jameson, who, while never regarded as an Althusserian, had nevertheless evinced sympathy for Althusser's project in the late seventies and early eighties, had similarly come increasingly to see Althusser and Macherey as crypto-postmodernists or irrationalists, who, whatever their stated commitment to Marxism, had contributed to the "randomization" of history.

In the face of such widespread condemnation and, more damningly, disinterest, it would seem that the present study could have no more important task than merely justifying its topic: Althusser and literary theory. Even to engage in such a justification, however, requires that we somehow free ourselves in whole or in part from the interpretative grid which imposes itself between us and the texts of Althusser and his co-thinkers. Althusser himself spoke of this problem in the process of attempting to read Marx's *Capital* in a genuinely new, unprecedented way. He became aware of the ways in which the same text gives rise to radically different interpretations in different historical periods, the ways that texts appear to select and offer up different parts of themselves according to historical imperatives that, more often than not, determine a reader's reading unawares. Paradoxically, then, the only way to say something new about Marx's text, to do more than read other readers (themselves reading other readers ad infinitum), is to begin by acknowledging that *Capital* has already been read for us and to grasp what that reading is that awaits us on every page: what does it call our attention to and what does it divert us from in *Capital*? What in Marx's text is as unreadable to us as if it had been deleted? Finally, what is at stake, politically and philosophically, in this game of visibility and invisibility?

But how can we even become fully aware of the reading that is imposed upon us, let alone escape it to produce a reading that is genuinely new? Althusser argued that one must set aside the myth of the solitary reader whose mind, if open (if it unburdens itself of the untested opinions of previous readers in the manner of Descartes), finds before it a text visible and readable in its entirety, if one is sufficiently attentive. Against this myth, Althusser argued that "there is no such thing as an innocent reading" (Althusser 1975; 13), that we genuinely begin to read a text by acknowledging and reading the readings that are imposed on us. "Imposed" is, of course, a strong word: it suggests more than that certain interpretations are, if not exactly inescapable, then unavoidable – and not simply because they are the most common, those shared by the greatest numbers of readers whose opinions have been widely disseminated. "Imposed" implies a certain use of force, the idea that interpretations are not simply a matter of an individual's free use of reason but are themselves subject to power relations that both privilege certain readings and simultaneously exclude or marginalize others. To follow Althusser's argument, then, we must cease to speak of the most common or the most widely shared interpretations of given works and speak instead of dominant interpretations, of interpretations that are widely shared because certain relations of force and power determine them to be so. If anything, a recognition of this fact makes the task of reading Althusser all the more daunting. If the dominant interpretation of Althusser is not merely widely shared or even accepted by readers free to make up their own minds about the meaning of the texts but is dominant to the extent that it is imposed through institutions and their rituals and practices, there can no longer be any question of "refuting" or "rebutting" this interpretation. One does not refute rituals, one diminishes their frequency and their effects in a given society.

But what rituals impose meaning on us and on the texts we read, we who live in free societies and not, after all, theocracies? In fact, without going into detail, it is sufficient to point out that the reading of works like Althusser's seldom takes place in solitude; most often these works are read in classes in colleges and universities where they are "required" or "mandatory" reading in a specific class. Students read these texts with the aid of an instructor, who will offer them the wherewithal to make sense of these difficult works, a meaning or set of meanings that may safely be substituted or exchanged for the work itself. It is this meaning that must be furnished on demand during the ritual known as the examination, a ritual which as Foucault remarked is not so much designed to make all individuals the same or make them think the same way, as to plot the degree of their deviation from a norm, in this case, a norm of knowledge. Students will be asked to summarize Althusser's thought, that is, what in it is essential and what less so and to classify it, to locate Althusser in the taxonomy that governs the field in which his work is to be situated (structuralism, literary theory, Marxism, etc.). Of course, if, as is often the case, the instructor should not entirely succeed in communicating the meaning of Althusser's work, there exist numerous "secondary works" (like the present study) that will present this meaning in a more comprehensive and accessible form. Such commentaries both inform and are written by academic experts. If, however, there can be no question of simply "setting aside" the dominant reading, how can we escape its hold? A first step, itself made possible by historical and cultural developments that have disrupted and destabilized the domination of the dominant reading of Althusser, must consist of clearly identifying and analyzing this reading.

To review the secondary literature on Althusser is to discover that there is more than one identifiable Althusserianism and that these divergent readings vary according to discipline. Thus, E. P. Thompson's ferocious attack on Althusser in *The Poverty of Theory* enjoyed considerable success in the social sciences (especially history and sociology) perhaps because his charge that Althusser had done away with "agency," that is, with the idea that human individuals can transcend social conditions consciously to determine their own actions, coincided with a renewal of methodological individualism and rational-choice theory even among self-described Marxists in these fields. Many theoreticians felt that explanations, as opposed to descriptions, of social phenomena must seek out the origins of these phenomena in the conscious choices of individuals. More importantly, however, British Althusserianism in social theory had already begun to collapse under the weight of its own contradictions; its main practitioners Barry Hindess and Paul Hirst had moved away from both Althusser and Marxism after less than a decade. Their attempts to construct a science of history out of a set of concepts extracted from Althusser, beginning with the journal *Theoretical Practice* and culminating very rapidly in such collective works as *Mode of Production and Social Formation,* foundered after no more than five or six years of effort. Ted Benton's *The Rise and Fall of Structural Marxism: Althusser and his Influence* represented the voice of moderation in the mid-1980s. He spoke for all those who continued to find Althusser valuable, and defended him valiantly against Thompson. Benton, however, clearly viewed Althusser's "structural Marxism" as having "fallen" and been reduced to rubble. His was an attempt to reconstruct from the wreckage of Althusser's work an Althusserian system which, although different from and far more structuralist than the system offered by Hindess and Hirst (indeed, Benton is quite critical of their reading of Althusser), shared with them the effort to shape Althusser's work into a coherent explanatory system, an effort that necessarily meant selecting certain elements and ignoring or setting aside others. In both cases, however, the systems these thinkers built from the materials provided by Althusser appeared faulty and were discarded as failures.

What is significant for our purposes, and indeed striking today in its own terms, about these influential commentaries is their distance from Althusser's actual texts, the extraordinary proportion of summary to citation, their tendency to present arguments abstracted from the actual form they take in Althusser's work. There was, of course, nothing unusual about such a procedure, especially in the social sciences where an emphasis on the textual existence of arguments could only be derided as exegesis instead of analysis. It happens, though, to fly in the face of everything Althusser taught and helps to account for the fact that today one cannot help but feel in reading Althusser that these commentaries, positive and negative alike, all refer to something other than Althusser's texts, a system or systems built from certain of the concepts or terms found in them, but not the texts themselves.

Interestingly, these battles raged nearly unnoticed in literary and cultural studies, where one only rarely encounters references to Hindess and Hirst or to Thompson. In part, this serene indifference suggests an insularity from other disciplines. Literary theory is attacked from all sides today as imperialist; it is said to move into any territory it desires without respecting the jurisdiction of other disciplines. From Habermas to Sokal, critics charge that literary theory reserves the right to speak about anything and in doing so reduces everything to the status of literature, that is, fiction. Such a view echoes Perry Anderson's charge of a quarter-century earlier that as Marxism's center of gravity shifted from Russia and Eastern Europe to Central and Western Europe and from professional political activists to academics and literati, Marxist theory had begun to turn away from politics and history and towards the referentless realms of philosophy, far from the struggles of social reality. Could it be then that Althusser continued to figure in literary and cultural theory, after ceasing to figure in the discussions and debates proper to the social sciences, precisely because the former is a realm of rhetoric rather than reason where the aesthetics of an argument, its ornamentation (which varies with fashion), matters more than its truth?

I will take a position diametrically opposed to the one outlined above; if Althusser has remained relevant to the study of literature, his relevance derives not from an indifference to truth but from the way in which his work has clarified some of the concrete problems that inevitably confront anyone who seeks to explain literature historically (and by this I do not mean simply explaining particular literary texts, but the very emergence in history of something called literature). Further, what is it that allows us *a priori* to judge the study of literature or culture as secondary or even inessential? Is it not possible that in the study of literature certain problems of historical explanation appear more clearly than in other fields?

The reading of Althusser that dominates literary theory takes the form not of a single, agreed-upon interpretation but rather of a dialectical union of opposing interpretations. Their unity derives from the fact that the one is the inverse of the other and their apparent opposition only confirms the sense that the alternatives they offer exhaust, or at least summarize, the possible readings of Althusser undeniably derived from two sources whose opposition only consolidates their domination. They appear as the two alternatives, the two interpretive choices that inescapably confront anyone who would read Althusser. In part, they offer normative judgments of his work, one positive, the other negative, but they do not merely hold his texts against an abstract standard, a set of axioms which Althusser will then be commended for following or condemned for ignoring; they also advance analyses of what he actually says. These alternative interpretations cannot be strictly identified with an individual commentator, or even a school of commentary: the last quarter-century of literary theory has seen far too many shifts in perspective, changes of heart, statements of regret, repudiation and rejection to rely on the putative continuous identity of the author. For brevity's sake, however, we can identify these opposing readings with two individuals insofar as we regard them as the authors of certain influential texts, and ignore for the moment the fact that they might later have modified or even dramatically changed their views. After all, it was not the inventor of deconstruction, but Plato himself who noted that written works can so easily turn against their progenitor, not only saying things that he never authorized them to say and circulating indiscriminately among those ignorant of the author and the truth he sought to convey, but returning to remind the author that he was once other than he is now and that that other has produced effects that he cannot control.

The first, positive, reading of Althusser (and Macherey) heralded *For Marx* and *Reading Capital*, as well as *Pour une théorie de la production littéraire*, as having inaugurated a scientific approach to literature. It is an important fact in the reception of Althusser that the translation of his works was accompanied, while Macherey's was preceded, by texts that did not so much comment on or interpret their ideas as offer an Althusserian system. This system, undeniably built with materials taken from his works and those of his students, nevertheless differed in crucial ways from that which it imitated. Interestingly, the most Althusserian work in Anglophone literary theory cites Althusser only rarely and Macherey only a bit more: Terry Eagleton's *Criticism and Ideology* (first published in 1976) – a work, like so many from this period, that enjoyed great success and influence only later to be disavowed by its author. Further, however much it differs from the work of Althusser and Macherey, and whatever the degree to which its project deviates from theirs, *Criticism and Ideology* exhibited a rigor and a commitment to historical knowledge that isn't often seen in literary studies. Moreover, irrespective of one's individual response to the work today, a quarter-century after its appearance, it must be acknowledged that Eagleton's text produced very powerful effects and contributed to a recasting of the discipline. His critique of both the crude philistinism of British Marxist approaches to culture and the empty aestheticism or moralism of the liberal humanist tradition, opened the way to a knowledge for which literature was both material and historical, a knowledge that the present work attempts to develop. By the mid-1980s, however, he too felt it necessary in his retrospective work *Against the Grain* (published in 1986) to take his distance from Althusser and Macherey, whose work, he argued, belonged to a structuralist moment that had long since passed and whose political effects were overwhelmingly negative, a case that subsequent works have stated in an even more emphatic manner.

Our object here, however, is not to trace the effects of *Criticism and Ideology* on the field of literary theory as a whole or even on Marxist literary theory as a sub-field, but to determine the way it constructed a powerful and highly influential model of Althusserian literary theory that both supplanted and obscured the theses advanced by Althusser and Macherey. It is extraordinarily instructive to set *Criticism and Ideology* next to Macherey's *Towards a Theory of Literary Production,* a work Eagleton had so thoroughly assimilated that even his style, so different from the laconic and far less serious (in every sense) approach he would adopt a decade later, resembled Macherey's Pascalian rhetoric, with its use of epigrams, its careful crafting of each sentence, its tendency to think in bursts, even fragments, even as it projected for itself the task of setting Marxism on the road to scientificity. But this continuity of style and terminology concealed some fundamental differences, particularly differences in scope. Macherey's text (although fifteen years after its appearance the author would describe it as "naïvely ambitious") begins by analyzing the most effective theoretical obstacles to a theory of the causes of literature and then moves directly to an analysis of a body of texts, primarily those of a decidedly non-canonical author, Jules Verne. What is conspicuously absent is the precise theory or method to which the bulk of *Criticism and Ideology* is devoted. Macherey here follows the example of Spinoza, whose practice he would later describe as a theoretical system or method that can never precede knowledge but can only reflect or express it, that must be practiced before it can be stated.

Eagleton's work proceeds in the inverse fashion: after a brief discussion of the history of "critical ideology," that is, the ideology of prior literary criticism in Britain, Eagleton proceeds to enumerate the "categories," "structures" or "elements" (Eagleton uses these terms interchangeably) whose combination produces the "object of literary theory," the text: the General Mode of Production, the Literary Mode of Production, General Ideology, Authorial Ideology and Aesthetic Ideology. The science of the text will thus be the study of the specific forms in which these elements combine, their hierarchical articulation. Thus, the General Mode of Production will determine both the Literary Mode of Production and the General Ideology. The General Ideology will in turn determine the Authorial and Aesthetic Ideologies. Each of these elements is itself a set of elements, a menu of possibilities, a fact that makes literature considered as the set of all texts, an infinitely open field of potential combinations. In this way, Eagleton appears to have constructed a formal system that precedes historical reality as its ideal condition of possibility. Such is not the case, however: not only is literature determined by the circumstances of its production as a material artifact, even the system of the General Ideology within which both Authorial and Aesthetic Ideology take shape is in no way a closed system, an ideal combinatory. It has a "referent," namely History, without which it could have no meaning. If ideology has, as Althusser insisted, a practical existence, if it is a kind of practice, it is a "signifying practice," a system of significations whose meaning finally derives from a referent external to it, the historical Real which is, as often as not, present in Ideology only in its absence. Reading the work today, one cannot entirely escape the feeling that, despite its Althusserian lexicon, the theoretical system offered in *Criticism and Ideology* is much closer to the "Marxism" of Lévi-Strauss's *Structural Anthropology* than to anything Althusser or Macherey wrote.

A second, negative, reading of Althusser and Macherey took shape a mere eight years after the publication of *Criticism and Ideology* and it crystalized around the work of Fredric Jameson. Interestingly, in *The Political Unconscious* published in 1981, Jameson viewed Althusser and Macherey with a great deal of sympathy as a superior form of structural Marxism, which could acknowledge the heterogeneity of literary texts but then required

> this multiplicity to be reunified, if not at the level of the work itself, then at the level of its process of production, which is not random but can be described as a coherent functional operation in its own right. The current post-structural celebration of discontinuity and heterogeneity is therefore only a moment in Althusserian exegesis, which then requires the fragments, the incommensurable levels, the heterogeneous impulses of the text to be once again related, but in the mode of structural difference and determinate contradiction. (Jameson 1981, 56)

Even Jameson's evocation of Althusser/Macherey against the critique of totalization he associated first with Deleuze and Guattari's *Anti-Oedipus* and later with postmodernism exhibits some important contradictions. In keeping with the project of a Marxist hermeneutics that Jameson advances in *The Political Unconscious,* he reads Althusser and Macherey as practicing an exegesis, describing the disorder in any text only then to demonstrate it as a function of a superior order, a "coherent functional operation" (ibid., 56). Functional operations, of course, do not produce contradictions, they resolve them. All that exists within them, exists to reproduce their equilibrium. In the next sentence, Jameson counterposes mere difference and heterogeneity to "structural difference and determinate contradiction" (ibid., 56). Presumably, by the latter phrases, Jameson seeks to denote those differences and contradictions to which a Marxist hermeneutic procedure could be applied. How does a Marxist hermeneutic differ from the traditional model of interpretation? It does not regard the text as the expression or reflection of a reality external to it according to a vertical model, but grasps it, horizontally, as it were, as the individual actualization of a broader system of ideology whose basic units, called ideologemes, combine in various ways to produce meaningful statements. By a different, far less direct route, and employing a markedly less Althusserian vocabulary, Jameson arrived at a theory of the text nearly identical to Eagleton's (whose *Criticism and Ideology* Jameson never cites).

Jameson, of course, never identified with Althusserianism in the way that Eagleton did and took his distance from Eagleton, Macherey and Althusser for a reason. Even his sympathetic discussion of Althusser and Macherey exhibits a certain uneasiness or anxiety; their work appears to contain a certain destabilizing element that he cannot ever quite explain away. Perhaps the phrase "determinate contradiction" in association with Althusser's name inescapably refers to his essay "Contradiction and Overdetermination," in which he takes great pains to show that historical contradictions are never part of a larger unity except in the temporary sense of "a vast accumulation of 'contradictions'" which come into play "in the same court, some of which are radically heterogeneous – of different origins, different sense, different levels and points of application – but which nevertheless merge into a ruptural unity" (Althusser 1969, 100). Althusser repeats the term "accumulation" frequently in describing the relation between the multiplicity of contradictions, as if to stress that in no way can this ruptural unity ever assume the form of a system. Thus, ten years before *Anti-Oedipus*, Althusser seems to have argued in the guise of a commentary on Lenin something remarkably similar to Deleuze and Guattari's critique of totalization, which in retrospect appears rather tame next to Althusser's 1962 text:

> We no longer believe in a primordial totality that once existed or in a final totality that awaits us at some future date. We no longer believe in the dull gray outlines of a dreary, colorless dialectic of evolution, aiming at forming a harmonious whole out of heterogeneous bits by rounding off their rough edges. We believe only in totalities that are peripheral. And if we discover such a totality alongside various separate parts, it is a whole of these particular parts but does not totalize them; it is a unity of all these particular parts but does not unify them; rather, it is added to them as a new part fabricated separately.
>
> (Deleuze and Guattari 1999, 42)

Three years after the publication of *The Political Unconscious*, Jameson would fire the opening salvo in the cultural battle over postmodernism, "Postmodernism or the Cultural Logic of Late Capitalism" in the *New Left Review*. His anxiety in the face of the emphasis on the heterogeneous and the multiple in French philosophy, already apparent in *The Political Unconscious*, had increased in scope and intensity, compelling him to redraw the political and theoretical boundaries of the present scene. While he concludes his essay with a favorable reference to the distinction between science and ideology as Althusser formulated it in his early work, Jameson found the source of the typically postmodern obsession with disorder and instability to be none other than Pierre Macherey: Macherey's work – for Eagleton, the foundation of "a science of the text" which would explain the way that certain pre-given elements combined to produce individual literary works – had become, for Jameson, a symptom of postmodern irrationalism. He reserves for Macherey, not for self-described postmodernists like Lyotard or Baudrillard, or even the deconstructionist Derrida (who often faces such charges), the distinction of having turned criticism away from the task of grasping the rational unity of works of art: "Our own recent criticism, from Macherey on, has been concerned to stress the heterogeneity and profound discontinuities of the work of art, no longer unified or organic, but now virtual grab-bag or lumber room of disjoined subsystems and random raw materials and impulses of all kinds" (Jameson 1984, 75).

At the time, more than one reader found Jameson's critique of Macherey and by extension Althusser untenable. Althusser remained for most readers, if not exactly a structuralist (after all, he had declared emphatically in his *Elements of Self-Criticism*, "we were never structuralists"), at least a philosopher committed to the defense of scientific knowledge against the claims of the relativisms and skepticisms of the twentieth century. Jameson's argument, however, proved prescient.

Much had happened in the world of Althusser and his circle in the years that separated Eagleton's *Criticism and Ideology* from Jameson's "Postmodernism." In November 1980, Althusser in one of the delusional states from which he had suffered most of his adult life, strangled his wife, Hélène Legotien. Although found to have been insane at the time he committed the crime and unfit to stand trial, Althusser spent most of the remaining ten years of his life in psychiatric hospitals. In the academic world internationally, apart from a handful of professional anti-Marxists who decided to exploit the tragedy to offer the equation "Marx equals murder," Althusser was referred to if at all in the past tense as if dead; it was assumed that, even if he remained physically alive, he was intellectually dead, incapable ever again of writing something Althusserian. Even before his death in 1990, however, there were signs that these assumptions were false. Amid little fanfare and unbeknownst to much of his audience, Althusser agreed to the publication in Spanish translation of a series of interviews conducted by a Spanish philosopher, Fernanda Navarro, in 1984. *Filosofía y marxismo* appeared in 1988 and held some surprises in store for the reader expecting a re-statement of Althusserian doctrine circa 1965 (or inversely, a recanting or repudiation of this doctrine, a genre particularly favored during this period by one-time Marxists). In the course of the interview, Althusser introduced not in opposition to Marxism but as the only philosophy adequate to it, the notion of an "aleatory materialism" ("aleatory" being derived from the Latin *alea*, for the dice or games of chance), a materialism according to which necessity emerges from the concatenation of chance encounters, and which thus rejects every notion of teleology. He identifies as the "sole materialist tradition," a lineage that embraces Epicurus, Lucretius, Machiavelli, Spinoza, Marx and Heidegger. In the light of this tradition, he tells us, the notion of historical or social laws appears meaningless; instead, we must understand history as conjuncture, which in turn "signifies conjunction, that is, the aleatory encounter of elements in part already in existence, but also in part unforeseeable. Every conjuncture is a singular case like all historical individualities, like all that exists" (Althusser 1994, 45–6).

After Althusser's death in 1990, it was learned that he had left behind an unpublished corpus that dwarfed the work published during his lifetime and which included over a dozen full-length manuscripts (including books on Hegel and Machiavelli, as well as the full-length book from which the essay "Ideology and Ideological State Apparatuses" – arguably Althusser's most influential work – was extracted) and perhaps a hundred essays in various stages of completion. Also recovered were the thousands of letters Althusser wrote to (and received from) such figures as Lacan, Barthes, Deleuze, Derrida, Foucault among others. Nearly four thousand pages of material has been published posthumously in the original French and less than a quarter of that in English translation. Tens of thousands of pages of material are gathered in an archive in Paris at the Institut Mémoires de l'Édition Contemporaine. Of all the materials recovered none was more surprising and provocative than a full-length autobiography, entitled *L'Avenir dure longtemps,* which begins with a minute reconstruction of the murder of his wife as he recalled it. The narrator (who better to insist on suspending any direct identification of the narrator with Althusser himself than those pursuing literary studies?) both merges with and diverges from the Althusser familiar to readers of *For Marx* or "Ideology and Ideological State Apparatuses"; he both is and is not the same voice. The autobiography has incontestably changed the way we read Althusser: it has illuminated certain passages in otherwise rigorous philosophy texts, passages whose beauty one might have admired even while regarding them as rhetorical embellishments. No one will ever read the following from the famous essay "Freud and Lacan" (1964) in quite the same way again:

> That this small biological being survives and not as a "wolf-child" that has become a little wolf or bear (as displayed in the princely courts of the eighteenth-century), but as a *human child* (having escaped all childhood deaths, many of which are human deaths, deaths punishing the failure of humanization), that is the test all adults have passed: they are the never forgetful witnesses, and very often the victims, of this victory, bearing in their most hidden, i.e., their most clamorous parts, the wounds, weaknesses and stiffnesses that result from this struggle for human life or death. Some, the majority, have emerged unscathed – or, at least give this out to be the case; many of these veterans bear the marks throughout their lives; some will die from their fight, though at some remove, the old wounds suddenly opening up in psychotic explosion, in madness, the ultimate compulsion of a "negative therapeutic reaction"; others, more numerous, as "normally" as you like, in the guise of an "organic decay". (Althusser 1971, 205)

L'Avenir dure longtemps is precisely Althusser's narrative of his own "human death," a narrative of the aleatory within the life of an individual, a life lived suspended over an abyss of emptiness and death. It is untrustworthy, a very tightly woven web of truths and falsehoods that simultaneously affirms and attempts to destroy Althusser's accomplishments. In any case, it, together with other writings from the 1980s published soon after his death, tempt us, following Jameson but going further than he, to identify another Althusser, an Althusser in every way opposed to the structuralist thinker he was supposed to be, an aleatory Althusser ever haunted by the void, the madman whose madness is his truth, a madman for whom truth is itself a kind of madness, a delusion by which we defend against the abyss that surrounds us. He could appropriate from Hegel the concept of the labor of the negative only to turn it against Hegel by making it irreducible, negation that cannot itself be negated or transcended, an Althusser for whom, as François Matheron has noted, the void (*le vide*: a term whose recurrence in Althusser's work from the beginning to the end of his career is not always visible in English translations) was a central concept.

Thus, a reading takes shape that is all the more powerful and persuasive in that it offers itself as a set of alternatives, a choice between opposing views whose very opposition makes the set appear exhaustive: Althusser the structuralist philosopher, the thinker of the formal orders of history, and Althusser the postmodernist poet, prophet of unreason, celebrant of difference and disorder: how may we explain the emergence of these two diametrically opposed and incompatible readings of the same body of work? If we take Althusser seriously there is one thing we cannot do: we cannot write these readings off as merely subjective projections onto the texts of Althusser and Macherey of what cannot be found within them. On the contrary, as Althusser said repeatedly, the truth of a philosophy is in its effects. These opposing readings are the effects of the texts in question. As Étienne Balibar has said, there will always be two kinds of Althusserians, "Althusserians of the Conjuncture and Althusserians of the Structure," precisely because this antagonism traverses his entire corpus (Balibar 1993a, 94). Are readers thus condemned to wander between these two perspectives, as if Althusser could not be seen but from these contrasting views?

Note

1. Throughout most of the 1960s Althusser worked very closely with a group of philosophy students from the École Normale Supérieure, most of whom, like Althusser, were also members of the French Communist Party, in a kind of theoretical and political collective. At the beginning, Althusser played the role of teacher; very rapidly, however, he found himself outpaced in certain ways by his colleagues and a genuine intellectual collectivity took shape. In 1964, he marveled to a correspondent, in the colloquial and familiar idiom of intimate conversation, that he was "absolutely blown away" by the work produced by these young people. "They have already read everything and have tons of ideas. They are literally kicking my ass, as we say in our crude language: I am behind them, I have to catch up (if I can!)." From the other side, Pierre Macherey in a recent look back at his years with Althusser, writes of having written until about 1975 under the direct influence of Althusser, in a situation of nearly total osmosis with his way of thinking (Macherey 1999, 5). He goes on to describe the years of his collective engagement with Althusser and others in terms that are both moving and theoretically pertinent to the present study: "I thus worked for more than a decade in close conjunction with Althusser and with some others who shared the same commitment: this was not haphazard star-worship.

With the passage of time that introduces moderation in all things, I will not hesitate to say that, in the limits of its irregular singularity, with its difficulties and its failures, not to speak of its dramas, it was an exhilarating experience in every sense: intellectually, politically and humanly. Althusser was a man of exceptional generosity (although the other side of this was perhaps what must be called his madness): I learned with him concretely what it was to share ideas, to have what Spinoza called common notions, an important aspect of the communism that we, no doubt with a great deal of naivete, wished for with all our hearts and whose coming we regarded as certain" (Macherey 1999, 6).

In the face of such statements, I can see little justification for artificially separating what, on the basis of textual evidence alone, ought to be regarded as a collective body of work whose writers functioned more as scribes than as authors, recording ideas that had so thoroughly circulated between individuals that their originator could no longer be discovered.

1 Towards a New Reading of Althusser

First encounters: art against ideology

"A childhood memory: those stories of explorers who come upon an immense river *without knowing where it leads.* They hollow out a log and entrust their craft to the current for months simply to discover the sea" (Althusser 1998, 386). So concluded a letter in the remarkable correspondence that Althusser carried on with Franca Madonia in the heady years of the 1960s. The letter is dated 6 March 1963, the middle of perhaps the most productive period in his life, the period in which he wrote his most influential books and essays. The passage gives us in the form of a myth a sense of the way Althusser conceptualized his own philosophical activity: neither patient, linear and progressive theory-building nor the construction of explanatory models (in the structuralist spirit of the time). In attempting to identify what was genuinely new and unprecedented in Marx, Althusser's orientation was to texts rather than to ideas or arguments abstracted from texts. To think was to explore what had already been thought and written, moving through the already-thought to take a position in it. Most philosophers took a position without being aware that they did so; Althusser, in contrast, sought to develop a theory of taking positions in philosophy. It was in this sense that he could speak of "cutting a path" through "the immense forests" of Marx's *Capital* (Althusser 1975, 14).

The very act of reading, the act of exploring the already-thought and the already-said, not, of course, to repeat it but to find what has already been said without our knowing that it has been said, that is, to discover a past that has never been fully present, a past deferred to the future, became, for Althusser, an activity full of adventure and risk: the risk of following a false path, a path that leads and can lead nowhere. To return to his parable: the risk of setting out on impassable rivers (and how can one know in advance that an uncharted river becomes unnavigable?), of following diverging branches for months or years only to find them disappear into the earth or empty into immense swamps, and the accompanying risk of becoming lost and disoriented, unable either to retreat or advance. Let us accordingly follow Althusser as he explores the river on which he set out, a river full of forks and tributaries, taking care to note not only his progress, but also the occasions on which he must retreat or seek a detour in order to find a way forward. Such an approach will allow us to set aside in advance the notion, common to Althusser's detractors and admirers alike, that his work as a whole is characterized by a fundamental unity and coherence. To read his work carefully, to the letter as he liked to say, is to retrace voyages on waterways that, however promising their beginnings, proved finally to be impassable; it is also, however, to rediscover rivers still open and unexplored before us, perhaps leading to seas still to be found.

We will begin with the following observation: what we have called Althusser's most productive period coincided with a new-found interest in contemporary painting and literature, particularly drama. This meant, among other things, that at the very moment he began radically and publicly to take his distance from the traditional Communist positions on philosophy, so he came to question what passed for a Marxist theory of art. We know little of the views he held on art during the 1950s or even whether he devoted much thought to it at all.[1] His correspondence with Franca Madonia, however, reveals that even by 1962 he had yet to abandon what she regarded as the "orthodox" line on avant-garde theater. In that year, she wrote

> I continue to read essays and articles against what is called "avant-garde theater" (it was one year ago that some friends, among them you, Hélène or Bernard,[2] still expressed your hostility to it). In effect, I have decided that you are all wrong and I say this to you because you seem more salvageable than the others. Of course, if one begins in art from the orthodox Marxist precept of the Eleventh Thesis on Feuerbach that it is not a matter of interpreting the world but of changing it, there is very little going on. (Althusser 1998, 202)[3]

Judged from this austere perspective, Madonia adds,

> all modern art (or most of it) in its diverse manifestations, painting,

> sculpture, poetry, music, etc. is to be rejected and it is true that orthodox Communist critics reject it en bloc. They do not ask whether a given abstract or informal element is better than some other, they refuse abstract and informal painting in itself, ignoring the importance or validity of the change that has taken place in the artistic milieu over the last ten years. (Ibid., 202)

For such critics, any failure to communicate in as direct a manner as possible the solution to the urgent social and political problems of the time must be condemned. An art whose form (or lack thereof) impedes or complicates the transmission of its essential content can only be condemned as a relapse into precisely the contemplative attitude that Marx's epigram would seem to condemn.

In opposition, Madonia argues that "a great revolution" has occurred but that "it is that which is situated at the level of form" (ibid., 202). For her, it is the form of Brecht's plays that "deprives consciousness of its character as a personal refuge" by abolishing the distinction between interiority and exteriority. Even the work of Beckett (who is "so different from Brecht") abolishes any internal drama, any drama of a consciousness that transcends the world and whose conflicts would remain independent of social and political struggles. She argues, quite strikingly, that Beckett's plays exhibit even in their minimalism a collectivity anterior to the consciousness of the individual even if that collectivity only appears as an absence, the empty horizon of Beckett's borderless spaces, the immense void that weighs on every word his characters utter and on every gesture they make. Thus, in opposition to portrayals of heroic masses, paradoxically almost always embodied in a single hero, Beckett's plays make us feel that collectivity that the individualist ideologies we daily live would have us deny by presenting to us a world devoid of the least suggestion of society but palpably not a state of nature, that is, not "the human condition" considered outside of history. One will miss this revolution in art if one views it from "a strictly communist point of view, that is the point of view of content alone" (ibid., 203). Madonia appeals to Althusser because "your acceptance of modern painting is the proof of the freedom I demand equally for the theater" (ibid., 203).

The interest in modern painting to which she refers and even the written expressions of this interest have not received the attention they deserve, despite the fact that one of Althusser's most important essays from this period, "Cremonini, Painter of the Abstract," was translated into English nearly thirty years ago. In 1964, on the occasion of his viewing Cremonini's work at the Venice Biennial Exhibition of that year, Althusser wrote an impassioned defense of the Italian painter, whose work had been dismissed as a derivative and tardy form of expressionism. His defense, importantly, is addressed not simply to the "technicians of taste," that is, the professional critics, but also, if less directly, to the "orthodox communist" critics to whom Madonia had referred in her letter. Without naming them or summarizing their rejection in principle of art that departs from a realist perspective, Althusser wrote that it is impossible

> to paint living conditions, to paint social relations, to paint the relations of production or the forms of the class struggle in a given society. But it is possible, through their objects, to "paint" visible connections that depict, by their disposition, the *determinate absence* which governs them. The structure which controls the concrete existence of men, i.e., which informs the lived ideology of the relations between objects and men, this structure as a structure, can never be depicted by its presence, in person, positively, in relief, but only by traces and effects, negatively, by indices of absence. (Althusser 1971, 237)

Madonia's remarks help us understand Althusser's growing interest in non-realist theater, art and literature in the 1960s and to situate it in relation to his philosophical project as a whole. Althusser's increasing distaste for realist art (whether socialist or merely social realism) was a consequence of his growing conviction that realism was based on the extremely naïve notion that reality lay before it waiting to be represented (whereas non-realist forms of art distorted or obscured this reality, impeding our ability clearly to see it); art, according to the well-known figure, would simply be the mirror held up to the world. In fact, what realist art and literature often mirrored was not reality but the themes and myths of the ideologies through which human beings lived their relations to historical reality. And of all the ideological myths none proved more tenacious (as much within Marxism as outside of it), as that of humanism, perhaps the *sine qua non* of capitalist society. In an essay written in 1963 at the request of the Marxist Humanist Erich Fromm (who was so disturbed by Althusser's essay that he rejected the piece that he himself had commissioned),[4]

Althusser defined philosophical humanism as constituted by two principles. First, "that there is a universal essence of man," and second, "that this essence is the attribute of 'each single individual'" (Althusser 1969, 228).

What does Althusser mean by "universal essence of man"? He refers to the idea that there exists a fixed human nature, outside of and prior to all history, which affects this history without itself being affected in return and is therefore that which explains but cannot itself be explained by history. There exist fundamentally different and even opposed theories of this nature: we need refer only to the debates in the eighteenth century between the exponents of a benevolent human nature and those who defended the notion of motivation by individual self-interest alone (which are repeated, often in less rigorous terms, among contemporary sociobiologists about whether human beings are naturally egoistic or altruistic). But underlying all these conceptions of human nature even in their divergence is what Althusser calls "the philosophical form of bourgeois ideology that has dominated history for five centuries":[5] the notion of the human individual as a conscious subject, that is, a self, conscious of its thoughts, needs and desires, and origin, and master of its words and deeds, and so distinct from other selves that the very existence of "other minds" could become a serious philosophical dilemma. This ideology declares individuals responsible for their acts (not only ethically responsible, of course, but also legally responsible and subject to punishment) and free (the worker voluntarily enters into a contract with the employer and his consent renders legitimate whatever conditions and hours he must endure; after all, no one forced him to take the job). These quotidian examples can be, of course, supplemented by more sublime versions. To take as an example a doctrine with which Althusser himself had to engage, existentialism: human beings are condemned to a freedom that they will do anything to deny; they invent Gods, Parties, Ideals all to escape the terrifying solitude of their essential condition, which is to make choices for which they themselves alone are responsible because they alone determine their actions.[6]

What Althusser called humanism governs to a very great extent the way we think about art and literature. Are not the very notions of artist and author (as they have functioned during the last two centuries), insofar as they serve to explain a given work or body of work, based on similar myths: the author "creates" a text which is an expression of his unique and private self and as such his property to dispose of as he sees fit? If we would understand the text, we would ask what in him explains it, his intention, conscious or unconscious, his life, etc. According to Althusser, those notions were precisely the most important obstacles to a rational apprehension of art, and thus the most urgent task for Marxism in his time was to "reduce to ashes" the "philosophical myth of man" (ibid., 229). He had already come to understand that the dismantling of this myth had been going on for some time in the work of the literary and artistic avant garde. It was thus his commitment to the cause of theoretical anti-humanism that allowed him to read in the formal disruption of minimalist theater, abstract expressionist painting and the most austere experiments in French New Wave cinema, not the subjectivist denial of social reality or elitist formalism of which they were accused by many Communist writers, but nothing less than an assault on the humanist foundation of bourgeois ideology, objectively (that is, independent of the intentions of the artist or author) far more radical than the productions of social realism, which began to seem mere variants of the ideology they claimed to oppose.

For Althusser the function of art was not so much to make reality visible as to make visible the myths that govern, without our knowledge or consent, the way we think about and "live" this reality. Art thus takes on a crucial role: only when the concepts of which ideology is fabricated are "displaced" (one might just as well say "deconstructed") will it be possible to think differently and set out on the road to a properly scientific knowledge of history. It was precisely this subversion of the ideology of the subject that attracted Althusser to the art of Leonardo Cremonini. In his paintings, according to Althusser, there are no objects, places, moments, or even people. The familiar world of discrete individual objects and beings with its distinctions between the animate and the inanimate, between nature and culture and therefore between the human and the natural is subjected to a process of decomposition. It is a world of eviscerated bodies indistinguishable from the rocks among which they are scattered, a world of skeletons already crumbling into the ground, from which they can barely be differentiated. Cremonini is "not an abstract painter but a painter of abstraction": he calls into question the transcendence of the human in relation to the natural and subtly dissolves every trace of spirit into brute matter. Men take on the form of things:

> "Bodies and faces of stone, revealing in their objects and gestures their primordial origins: precisely those bones transposed into tools, those thin elbows articulated into the arms of chairs, those women erect like the iron balustrades of their balconies. . . . The "men": fashioned from the material of their objects, circumscribed by it, caught and defined once and for all: faces corroded by the air, gnawed and seemingly amputated (almost too much faces), gestures and cries congealed into immutable weight, a parody of human time reduced to eternity, the eternity of matter. (Althusser 1971, 234)

Even after 1961, when the human figures in Cremonini's paintings become more rather than less distinct, there is no return to a figural humanism: Althusser notes that "only a few years ago," the painter began an exploration of mirrors, and therefore an exploration of the relations of individuals to themselves: his figures do not

> look at themselves, nor are they looked at. It is their mirrors, their wretchedness which fastens them, restoring to them despite themselves, whatever they do, their only inalienable possession: their own image. . . . Those women at the dressing table do not see themselves though they look at themselves in the mirror, even that young woman does not see herself, though we see her naked desire on the back of the looking-glass she holds in her hand: it is their mirrors that see them, and see the circle of their sight, though the mirrors are blind. (Ibid., 235)

Cremonini's figures look into the mirror but do not see themselves, or they are seen without seeing themselves in mirrors: in his paintings there is no origin, no center except perhaps that deferred and displaced beyond the boundaries of the canvas. They are lost to themselves, subject to the impossibility of ever being subjects. This is the sense in which Cremonini is "not an abstract painter, but a painter of abstraction," painting impossibility itself. He does not render these figures as they are, but as they are not, painting the lack that defines them and makes them what they are.

Althusser saw in the avant-garde theater of the 1950s and 1960s an even greater destabilizing of humanist ideology. In fact, his exchange with Madonia on the subject of art had begun with his report of having attended a production of Carlo Bertolazzi's *El Nost Milan* on June 15, 1962. A little less than a month later he reported having finished an essay the rough draft of which Madonia had read and criticized. "The Piccolo: Bertolazzi and Brecht (notes on a materialist theater)" appeared in the journal *Esprit* in December of 1962; a few years later Althusser would reprint it in *For Marx.* Interestingly, the essay received little scholarly attention until recently. Balibar has gone so far as to argue that "The Piccolo" is the "veritable geometrical and theoretical center" of *For Marx,* but that it "figures in it as a 'purloined letter' in the sense that no one reads it as such, perhaps, shamefully, because it only concerns aesthetics and theater" (Althusser 1996, viii–ix, my translation). What then is this extraordinary essay, the overlooked center of a work that attempts to decenter history?

First, interestingly, Althusser did not have the text of the play before him; not that editions of Bertolazzi's *El Nost Milan* did not exist, but the production that Althusser attended departed in many ways from the author's 1893 play.[7] The avant-garde director, Giorgio Strehler, had condensed the original four acts into three and taken liberties with Bertolazzi's set directions. Typically, Althusser's analysis begins not with his experience of the play, as if that experience occurs in a vacuum, but with a quick survey of the context in which his experience takes place. By the second sentence of his essay Althusser has cited eight deprecatory remarks from six Parisian newspapers and journals. He has surveyed the critical response to the French production and finds that the critics have reached consensus: *El Nost Milan* is a minor melodrama, a cheap tear-jerker. He cannot pretend to ignore this judgment; on the contrary, he takes it with him to the theater. In doing so, he finds that it is not wrong, in the sense that critics have attributed to the work a property or properties that it does not possess, and that their reaction is not subjective, arising in and pertaining to them alone, but objectively determined by the play itself. What they have failed to see, what they have overlooked, is the fact that the play "criticizes" melodrama as an ideology and as a form of consciousness, not in so many words, of course, but in its very structure by removing the melodrama from the center and by forcing the audience to feel the emptiness of the place where this center should be. The audience then, at least the cultivated Parisian audience wrapped in melodrama itself, expecting and demanding nothing less than a "good" melodrama, could only experience this decentering as a flaw: the play is not only melodrama, it is bad melodrama.

The play consists of three acts and centers on three main characters. In the first act, set in Milan's Tivoli amid the bustle of the circus,

Nina, the fire-eater's daughter, is seen gazing longingly at Rico, the clown, when quickly the neighborhood tough, Carleou (the Togasso), attempts to accost her but is rebuffed. The interaction is witnessed by Nina's father. The second act (in Strehler's production: he omitted Bertolazzi's second act) takes place in a huge, half empty "Cucine Economiche," or soup kitchen. Although there are a number of characters on stage, seated at long tables eating silently in solitude or talking with others, they occupy only a small part of the stage. The audience is made to feel a sense of empty space, a space too great for them to fill. Nothing of significance happens for most of the act; near the end, Nina and her father enter, followed quickly by Carleou. The two men begin to quarrel over Nina (who has by this time succumbed to the addresses of Carleou), Carloeu pulls out a knife and the father wrestles it away, stabbing and killing him. All of this happens in the last two minutes of the act. The third and final act in Strehler's production is set in a women's shelter populated by a few abandoned elderly women and, halfway through the act, Nina. A few minutes from the play's end, her father enters, and announces that he has killed Carleou (and that he did it for her, to free her from her tormentor and corruptor) and will go to prison for his crime. Instead of the gratitude he expects, she erupts in anger. Nina denounces her father's ridiculous sense of honor and announces that she will do whatever she can to leave the life of poverty, including selling herself. Her father leaves, crushed, and she turns away, defiant.

It is very clear from the outset that Althusser understands *El Nost Milan* through Brecht. It is Brechtian theater that allows us to read the play not as melodrama but as a profound critique of its presuppositions. Althusser is fascinated by the organization of time in the play, particularly by the way in which nothing of consequence, nothing that is necessary to the development of the narrative, transpires during the greater part of each act. The events necessary to the development of the plot take place only at the end of each act, and only after the audience has been made to wait, been made impatient by the imposition of insignificant characters and empty dialogue. As Althusser notes, of the forty characters who take the stage, only three really matter and their words and actions occur in a flash, after long periods of empty time, without warning and without immediate consequence. The organization of time has its corollary in the organization of space. The important characters and their interactions often occupy a corner of the stage. Further, they are dwarfed by crowds in the first act and by empty space in the second and third. The effect of the play's spatial and temporal organization is a profound decentering. We are made to feel and to see the weight of emptiness on diminutive lives, of anonymous crowds on individuals. We feel the passage of a time in which nothing happens and nothing is said in a world where no honor is possible, not even through sacrifice because even sacrifice is deprived of meaning; it is a world whose truth is "silence, immobility and nothingness" (Althusser 1969, 136). But at the margins of this empty time, argues Althusser, another time erupts, a full time, the time of the event, a time of irreversible action in which lives change or end in an instant, by means of an action on which everything is staked. *El Nost Milan*, then, does not gather the fragments and pieces of the lives it exposes into a coherent whole; on the contrary, it represents the world by dissociating it from itself, by dividing it into two worlds between which there is no relation. For Althusser,

> it is precisely this opposition that gives Bertolazzi's play its depth. On the one hand, a non-dialectical time in which nothing happens, a time with no internal necessity forcing it into action: on the other, a dialectical time (that of conflict) induced by its internal contradiction to produce its development and result. The paradox of *El Nost Milan* is that the dialectic in it is acted marginally, so to speak, in the wings, somewhere in one corner of the stage and at the ends of acts. . . . This dialectic always appears after everyone has departed. (Ibid., 137–8)

History and reality are thus offstage, the world that Nina will enter when the play is done, the world out there. What is the world of the play and its characters, their actions and speeches? Quite simply a world of illusions, particularly the illusions of consciousness which imagines itself free and master of itself, the center and first mover of the world. Nina will leave this world of illusory freedom for a world of necessity. No character states this fact, no action reveals it; Bertolazzi more likely than not did not intend to imbue the play with this meaning and the audience does not directly grasp it even as it applauds at the curtain's closing. It is the structure of the play, the work of dissociation and divergence that it carries on. *El Nost Milan* is not about a reality, even the reality of Milan's sub-proletariat at the turn of the century; it is rather and most profoundly a critique of the dominant form of consciousness, melodramatic and moralizing, from the point of view of which, history must remain invisible.

To explicate more fully what he calls "the structure of the dialectic in the wings" (*la structure de la dialectique à la cantonade*), Althusser turns to "the great plays of Brecht," the most important of which for him will be *Galileo.* Far more than Brecht's explicitly theoretical writings, his plays work relentlessly to dissociate the apparent unity and coherence of the world and to make visible its "unresolved alterity": the inescapable opposition between time as experienced by consciousness, which imagines itself to be the agent and thus center of its progress, and a decentered time which, subject to the variability of the event and the encounter, is as likely to move backwards as forwards: light is edged by darkness, and every promise hints at a threat (at the extreme, the greatest boon to humankind may presage its obliteration). The coexistence of these two times in a single structure which juxtaposes without unifying them proves so discordant and jarring to the audience that there emerges "the basis for a true critique of the illusions of consciousness" (ibid., 142). In *Galileo,* these illusions are legion: Galileo the discoverer, the agent and subject of scientific progress is revealed in the first five minutes of the play not to have discovered the telescope at all but to have copied it from the description by a traveler just returned from Amsterdam (where, significantly, it is already widely diffused, its origins lost in anonymity – it has no inventor nor discoverer: only the masses make history) and moreover to have sold it as his "own" (his "intellectual property" as we would say today) for a tidy sum. Galileo is greedy, a glutton and an epicure, in fact; one cannot think on an empty stomach, without adequate spirits to stimulate the brain. Further, he is a coward, he recants before the Inquisition rather than martyr himself for the cause of science. His weaknesses and failings, however, matter little: scientific knowledge requires neither heroes nor prophets, its work is anonymous and collective, most often behind the backs of its practitioners, rarely taking center stage, gathering instead silently in the wings.

But Brecht is not Adam Smith: no invisible hand weaves harmony out of the threads of human discord. There is no necessary progress in his world: the same telescope that allows us to see the stars gives one army a tremendous advantage over another. In war, advantage means only one thing: death, death on a grand scale (just as during Brecht's time the most innocent discoveries in the field of nuclear physics quickly yielded a weapon that could destroy the entire human species in an instant). Perhaps most disturbing of all is the final scene of *Galileo*: as Galileo's protégé, Andrea, is about to smuggle a manuscript out of Italy and the hands of the Inquisition, he witnesses a group of boys throwing stones at the house of an old woman, of whom they have seen nothing but shadows but whom they have labeled a witch. Andrea lifts one of the boys up to a window allowing him to see that the witch is merely an old woman preparing her dinner. It is the act of science incarnate, replacing ignorance with knowledge and removing the conditions for superstition and hatred. As he turns to board the vessel that will take him and his manuscript to freedom, he hears the boys running back to the house to kill the witch. Brecht has exposed the most painful lesson a Marxist and a revolutionary can learn: that truth has very little force against superstition and ideology. The fantasy of the omnipotence of truth, as Althusser called it, is one of the most common illusions of consciousness. This would prove to be one of the key themes of Althusser's entire corpus.

For Brecht, Althusser writes,

> self-consciousness total, transparent, mirror of the entire drama is never anything but an image of ideological consciousness which includes the whole world in its drama, but only to the extent that the world is the world of morality, politics and religion, in short, of myths and opiates. It is in this sense that these plays are decentered precisely because they can have no center, because, starting from naive consciousness stuffed with illusion, Brecht refuses to make it the center of the world he would like it to be. That is why in these plays the center is always to one side, if I may put it that way, and insofar as it is a matter of a demystification of consciousness, the center is always deferred, always beyond, in a movement of advancing beyond illusion towards the real. (Ibid., 144–5, translation modified)

Althusser goes on to argue that even such notions as the alienation effect, at least as commonly understood, do not capture what is revolutionary about the theater of Brecht and Bertolazzi. The alienation effect is too often thought to be engendered by means external to the drama itself: the exposed machinery, the visibility of sets, the absence of costumes and a certain flat, pathosless style of acting. Understood in this way, any play could be staged in such a way as to produce an alienation of the spectators, who, even in the face of *King Lear*, would find themselves unable to suspend their disbelief and turn off their critical faculties. Althusser, in contrast, seeks to show that the alienation effect is inscribed in the plays themselves,[8] particularly in their decenteredness, in the fact that their center is always deferred until after the end. In part, the absence of a center, of a point from which all the elements of the play can be gathered together or at least seen and understood, is expressed in the absence of a hero. Thus, it is not only that Galileo lies, cheats and steals and not for science, but to feed his already ample belly, it is also and more importantly that he is not the origin of knowledge, neither discoverer nor inventor. But even the absence of heroes is insufficient to explain the alienation effect. Instead, it is the dissociated structure of the plays themselves that makes heroes impossible, insofar as this structure makes impossible any notion of a central consciousness, a consciousness possessed of an adequate knowledge of the dilemmas, moral and political, that it confronts and free to choose a course of action to resolve them. No character possesses this knowledge and neither does the audience. At this point Althusser rejects "the two classical models of spectatorial consciousness" that dominate our thinking about theater and art more generally (ibid., 148). First, the model of the self-conscious spectator who does not identify with the characters, even the hero, and who remains fully outside the drama, intentionally keeping a distance that will allow him to judge what passes before him; this model, according to Althusser, is as illusory in its premises as that which guides the actors on stage: a consciousness assured of its autonomy and freedom, as well as of its ability to know itself and the world it inhabits.

If, however, we would attempt to theorize the complicity that inescapably links the spectator to the play, Althusser finds the notion of identification completely inadequate to the task:

> Rigorously speaking, the concept of identification is a psychological, or, more precisely, analytic concept. Far be it from me to contest the effectivity of psychological processes in the spectator seated in front of the stage. But it must be said that the phenomena of projection, sublimation, etc. that can be observed, described and defined in controlled psychological situations cannot by themselves account for complex behavior as specific as that of the spectator-attending-a-

> performance. This behavior is primarily social and cultural-aesthetic, and as such it is also ideological. (Ibid., 148–9)

Not only are spectators and actors united by the experience of the production, they are united by the institution or apparatus of the theater, a space organized according to rituals that enjoin speech or silence, movement or immobility. But the most important ritual of all is that of recognition: on the most profound level, actors and spectators are united

> by the same myths, the same themes which govern us without our consent, by the same spontaneously lived. Yes, even if it is the ideology of the poor par exellence, as in *El Nost Milan,* we still eat of the same bread, we have the same rages, the same rebellions, the same madness (at least in memory where stalks this ever-imminent possibility), if not the same prostration before a time unmoved by any history. (Ibid., 150)

Can we say then that a play is a mirror in which spectators recognize themselves and their reality? To take the example of Brecht's *Galileo,* as Althusser reads it, such a response is impossible: in the place where we expect to see ourselves and to recognize our reality, that is, the very center of the play, there is an empty place. The movement of the play is not towards the completion of an action, it is a movement of decentering and deferral that conducts the spectator not only beyond the drama but beyond himself. The incompleteness of the play, the absence of resolution, the lack of a conclusion are not merely negative; they all exercise a certain force. They seize upon our self-recognition and "displace it, push it off to the side, find it and lose it (*le prendre et le perdre*), leave it, return to it, expose it from afar to forces which are external – and so drawn out – that, like those wine-glasses broken at a distance by a physical resonance, it comes to a sudden end as a heap of splinters on the ground" (ibid., 150). To submit oneself to *El Nost Milan* or *Galileo* is to feel the walls of one's separateness and autonomy shattered, our center dispersed outward, scattered so far that there can be no hope and, if one has really abandoned oneself to the experience, no longer any desire of recovering it. "The play is the production of a new spectator": a spectator, no longer a person, but an assemblage irreducible to the juridical individual or legal subject.[9]

But has not Althusser, so well known for his love of provocation, gone too far? Has he not written and signed his name to an essay that expresses what he found when he looked into his heart to write? The final sentence of the essay, perhaps one of the most powerful Althusser has ever written, obliterates the distinction between author, actor, spectator, between drama and life, suggesting that his essay is the effect of the play, the play pursuing itself, its themes, its passions in him as in so many others:

> I return to myself and the question, sudden and irresistible, assails me: whether these few pages in clumsy and blind way are nothing more than this unknown play from a June evening, *El Nost Milan*, pursuing in me its unfinished meaning, seeking in me, despite me, all the actors gone and the sets cleared away, the *beginning* of its silent discourse. (Ibid., 152)

However powerful and thought-provoking Althusser's analysis of specific works by Brecht and Bertolazzi, one thing remains painfully obvious: nowhere does Althusser offer even the elements of a theory of literature or drama. On the contrary, it would appear that Althusser has singled out for analysis precisely those works, whether paintings or plays, which he regards as exceptional. Their exceptional status, as we have seen, is determined by their decentering effects, that is, their subversion of humanist ideology. It is this that differentiates them from the mass not only of "mediocre" works, but even of "great," "classic" works that remain dependent, if only in the last analysis, on this ideology, which may assert itself in the form of a hero or merely the human figure intact on a canvas. Such an analysis would merely have changed the content rather than the form of the "orthodox Communist" doctrine of art, a position one would hardly expect Althusser to take. In fact, in a published text that, because it only appeared in Italian in the Sunday "culture" supplement of a provincial Italian newspaper, remained unknown until recently, he acknowledges that it is not possible "to explain avant-garde theater without providing a valid explanation of all theater, not only the theater of the present but also the theater of the past" (Althusser 1964, 6).

Althusser's theory of theater (for it is nothing less than that) is surprising in many respects. It is the transcription of a presentation that Althusser made at the request of Il Teatro Minimo, an amateur theater group in the Italian province of Forli, to a decidedly non-academic audience. The circumstances of the text are important: they explain why it so differs from his other works on art and theater from the same period: its style is not only far more casual and less rigorous, more popular, than the other texts, but it is as ambitious and global as the other texts are, if read carefully, cautious or "prudent" (to use a word that Althusser valued), focused on specific works rather than general notions like art or theater. As schematic and vague as the text is (it may in fact have been a hasty improvization on Althusser's part), it makes visible the important contradictions in Althusser's attempts to think about art, simultaneously pointing even in its haste and lack of rigor in different directions: one which can lead precisely nowhere, an idealist dead end; the other, a pathway still open before us.

Althusser begins by telling his audience that his "presentation is devoted to the following question: 'Why Theater?'" (ibid., 5). Coming from Althusser such a question is, to say the least, surprising: he would argue in a series of lectures given in 1967 that philosophy does not answer such questions (Why does x exist? What purpose does it serve?), which properly speaking belong to the domain of religion. Further, posed in such a radically transhistorical if not ahistorical manner, it assumes the essential identity of something called "theater" throughout recorded history and therefore prevents us from approaching the concept of theater more critically and more historically. Fortunately, although Althusser does not entirely escape the logic of this question, neither does his response constitute a genuine answer to the question as posed. Thus, instead of determining why theater exists, he determines its structure, its conditions of possibility. Such a determination must start with the recognition that all theater belongs to the set of objects of consumption that we encounter in our daily lives. Not that it is typical of this set, but its very singularity can only be understood in relation to the common objects of consumption. By "common objects," Althusser refers to those "that will be consumed immediately, directly and without effort": if I am hungry I buy bread and eat it; if I am bored I can listen to the radio, watch television or go to the movies. Even theater can be a common object of consumption, "a certain type of common theater, especially those comedies which are primarily distractions," sources of amusement consumed or enjoyed as effortlessly as one consumes one's bread. The structure of simple consumption is itself simple: I want bread, I request it, there is a response to my request. The request and the response, argues Althusser, are "on the same level" (ibid., 5).

There exist, however, other "indirect" objects of consumption in which the relation between request and response is more complicated. Knowledge is one such object: its acquisition and enjoyment are never effortless; one does not know in advance the nature of what one is going to receive. Art, while an indirect object of consumption, is different from the others of this type in that the dislocation between request and response is inscribed in the work itself. There is a "distance internal to the theatrical object itself," a dissociation of the principal elements of the play that can take three possible forms: sublimation, destruction, or displacement. This general structure forms the condition of possibility of actually existing (or extant) drama, which cannot be understood in terms of some historical progression from the simple to the complex or a succession of dramatic forms corresponding to the world-views of the historical epoch in which they were written. Instead, he argues, all drama can be classified as belonging to one of four groups the relation between which is one of simultaneity; the groups, in principle at least, represent the four possible forms that a dramatic text may take.

The first is the "epic–tragic–classical," the theater of Aeschylus, Corneille and Racine. Althusser takes the example of Corneille's *Le Cid*: the play "speaks of" reality, the historical reality of the *Reconquista*, but does so in a way that does not "call into question the value of the combatants' feelings, does not submit this history or its facts to criticism" (ibid., 6). The play reflects upon the history it depicts by sublimating it, by representing it in an idealized form purified of any contradiction or conflict that might in turn lead to questions or doubts about the dominant versions of this history. The second possible form of theater also functions through a sublimation of the reality it represents: Althusser calls this form "modern or dramatic theater" (we shouldn't be misled by the term "modern"; he includes Euripides, along with Goethe and Schiller, in this category). In modern or dramatic theater the contradictions and conflicts of a given historical situation are represented only to be resolved in a fictional, ideal manner, such as the sacrifice of the hero (he gives the example of Goethe's *Egmont*, whose hero dies so that the Low Countries may be freed from Spanish domination in the sixteenth century). This type of theater distances itself and its audience from historical reality not so much to criticize it as to offer a solution "that is posed as a moral lesson" (ibid., 7).

The third form of theater, Althusser argues, is "more complicated" (ibid., 7) than the first two. This form includes most comedy, but more importantly, includes what is often called "theater of the absurd." It does not represent historical reality by sublimating it, but subjects part of this reality to a critique. Pirandello's theater, for example, "is a critical theater insofar as it proves that men's assumptions do not correspond to reality. . . . It is a critique of the illusions, of the ideals, of the dreams that men think they live but in reality live only in dreams" (ibid., 7). Because it reduces to nothing the entire world of illusions, this theater can be understood as operating by destruction. Ionesco's work offers an even more radical version of this critique, an anti-theater that offers a critique not only of the imaginary reality that mankind think they live but even of the means of representing this imaginary reality as imaginary: "everything is destroyed" (ibid., 6). At the extreme, "the destruction of the theater that occurs within Ionesco's theater becomes language's destruction of itself" (ibid., 8). Althusser cites the example of Ionesco's *The Lesson*, in which "common language is destroyed, leaving a kind of delirious language that gives us a purely verbal liberation" (ibid., 8). The theater of destruction, while critical of what is now clearly identified not as reality but as an imaginary realm we take to be real, can be said in its own way to resolve the contradictions it uncovers "in a destruction of the whole" (ibid., 9). Thus, although this theater does not overcome the contradictions of the world through sublimation and idealization, neither does it finally permit a genuine critical apprehension of the world, the absurdity of which appears as uncaused and therefore unchangeable; for Ionesco the absurd functions as a state of nature, the original and essential human condition.

Only the fourth form of theater, the "critico-realist or dialectical" form associated with Beckett and Brecht (and improbably, without any explanation on Althusser's part, Shakespeare), presents historical reality in its conflictuality and complexity without any attempt to reduce or overcome its conflicts. It functions through what Althusser calls in Italian *spostamento* or "displacement": it changes the disposition of elements in the play. It disrupts the teleological order of the narrative by refusing to conclude and decenters the action by refusing to position a hero as the agent of actions. The world of Beckett and Brecht is a world in which the human is dominated by the inhuman and this inhumanity is as much internal as external to human beings. Contrary to the overwhelming majority of Beckett's English-language commentators, who see in *Waiting for Godot* and *Endgame* a theater of the absurd, or an existentialist doctrine of the human condition as it is, independent of all social and political reality, Althusser insisted on the inescapability of the social in even the most extreme of Beckett's situations. Vladimir and Estragon (the two main characters in *Godot*) are tramps, itinerant farm workers whose destitution is social not natural, the emptiness of their world a historical result, not a transhistorical given. What once existed was destroyed; those who lived were killed: "Where are all these corpses from?" Vladimir asks Estragon. They are surrounded not by eternal silence, but by "all the dead voices" that murmur and rustle "like sand . . . like leaves . . . like ashes," the ashes of a world reduced to rubble, where the dead are piled in mountains, a world of war and holocaust (Beckett 1954, 40). Further, Vladimir and Estragon occupy a certain juridical category: they are what we now call "transients" (once, vagabonds), itinerant farm workers between jobs, living on pilfered crops and on the edge of starvation; they sleep in ditches in order to avoid being beaten by "them," the guardians of private property. The emptiness of their time is directly related to the dead time of Bertolazzi's characters, the dead time of those without property, the unemployed and the penniless, a time without significance or event.

What is extraordinary about Beckett is that what we might call the realist effects of his work are produced precisely by the placing of historical, social reality *à la cantonade*, in the wings, in the margins, offstage, so that we, faced with the catastrophic consequences (most often denied by the very characters who suffer them), must reconstruct their causes. Through the displacement carried out by Beckett's plays they not only confront us with the humanist ideology that we "live" as reality but they show that the very quest to define human nature as it is outside of and prior to society is a form of denial. They make visible these contradictions and problems without resolving them or even so much as pointing to resolution.

Despite its stated aim, "*Perché il Teatro*" does not offer a genuine theory of theater, that is, a theory that would explain the causes of theater in its historical existence. In part, Althusser's notion of the four types of theater resembles the formal combinatory he denounced in various structuralist writers: the enumeration of a finite set of possibilities (the four types) that not only reduces all theater to these types but, more importantly, cannot explain why one possible model rather than any other is actualized at a given time. But in an even more surprising sense, the entire theoretical apparatus is less a set of formal elements than a set of criteria for evaluating or judging works according to their degree of "criticality." Great art (not simply theater, but painting and literature as well) carries out a displacement of the ideology it presents to us and allows it not simply to be seen as ideology but to be felt or experienced as such. In the case of theater in particular, the critico-realist drama displaces us in relation to ourselves, in relation to the originary subjects we "know" we are, each enclosed in a world of which we are the center and prime mover.

What is striking about these propositions is that they recur almost verbatim in Althusser's definitions of the activity of philosophy from the same period. Is what remains unsatisfactory about these notions a result of Althusser's own "displacement," a movement that simultaneously philosophizes theater and theatricalizes philosophy, finally effacing the distinction between them? In restoring the value of critique to a certain type of avant-garde theater, he accords a certain practice of philosophy not only its material effects, but its grandeur and pathos as well. It is difficult not to read in Althusser's description of the "miracle of theater" (a miracle, he hastens to add, that is "rational and objective"), in which, if the audience truly participates, the actors "can surpass themselves" to create a moment of collective knowledge and joy that emanates from no one individual but circulates freely between actors and audience alike, abolishing the distinction between them and between art and life, his own experience of philosophy and the teaching of philosophy.

The argument emerging here would become explicit in an unfinished piece from 1968, "Sur Brecht et Marx," in which Althusser acknowledges that far from Marxist theory helping him understand theater, it was rather that "*El Nost Milan* played an important role in my research. Seeing *El Nost Milan* I was better able to understand certain important things in Marx's thought" (Althusser 1994b, 524). The essay (as far as it goes) is organized around the hypothesis that there exists "a kind of parallelism between Brecht's revolution in theater and Marx's revolution in philosophy" (ibid., 544). Both recognize the objective, historical existence of the field in which they seek to intervene; neither field can be dismissed as illusion or error, neither can be made to disappear or suppressed by an act of will. We cannot free ourselves from the historical situation of theater or philosophy and any change in these fields must follow from the taking of a position in the historically determined conjuncture of their present existence. In theater this means that Brecht cannot simply refuse the rules and conventions of drama. To do so, would be to fail to produce any effects at all. Instead, he must

> introduce certain changes within theater, within the "play" (jeu) of theater to produce certain new effects. "Play" must be understood in two senses. First, in the traditional sense of a theatrical play (the actors put on a "play"); theater is a fictional representation of reality. The play is not life, is not reality. What is represented in theater is not life in person, science in person, politics in person. If any of these is represented, it is because it is not *present.* But "play" must be understood in a second sense: theater allows for this "play" (in the sense that there is "play" in a door, a hinge, a mechanism). This means that theater is made in such a way that it contains a place of "play" in which these changes can be introduced. (Ibid., 544)

The very same year Althusser delivered a highly theatrical address to the Société Française de Philosophie, "Lenin and Philosophy," in which he described the activity of philosophy in very similar terms. In a letter to Madonia shortly before his presentation, he wrote that he planned to deliver "before the very indulgent, solemn and ancient" Society a "very drole" communication in which he would "tell them things that will simply render them speechless" and which would "completely change the rules of war and of philosophical strategy" (Althusser 1998, 758). In fact, he calculated his actions and words carefully and accurately; the effect was one of high drama.[10] The room was so packed with students that some members of the Society were denied entrance. Perhaps the rapt attention of the enthralled audience allowed him to surpass himself: in any case, he succeeded in moving Jean Wahl, president of the society and facilitator of the event, to interrupt him with an expression of outrage when he approvingly cited Lenin's description of professional philosophers as "flunkeys with diplomas." Althusser went on to argue that philosophy, like theater, cannot be suppressed; it is the perennial element in which scientific discoveries are attacked and defended, exploited for apologetic purposes or protected from exploitation. Because it will never disappear, one must possess an adequate knowledge of its "mechanisms" and of its functioning in order to say something new in philosophy and to produce effects. Despite the fact that we esteem its doctrines for their internal coherence, philosophy, like theater, is the site of a certain amount of play. It is this play between the elements of philosophy that allows one "to effect a displacement" within it, given that both

> theater and philosophy are fundamentally determined by politics but devote all their efforts to efface and deny this determination in order to appear to have escaped politics. Brecht and Marx both in their own way seek to bring about a displacement, a dislocation in theater and philosophy that makes them speak about precisely what they deny: their relations to politics. (Althusser 1994b, 547)

Towards a theory of the materiality of art

We have now reached the impasse: Althusser has produced, as we suggested earlier, a quite orthodox theory of art. It divides art into two camps: the first, which includes most of what is written, staged and painted, is only the semblance of art. In fact, it is mere ideology reproduced, represented, restaged, in a word, repeated. Insofar as it is reducible to the ideology that it uncritically and unproblematically expresses this "art" does not merit analysis; the gesture of denunciation will suffice. It requires neither explanation nor interpretation because it has no specific existence, no substantiality: it is nothing more than ideology. The other art, genuine art, begins with ideology (especially, as we have seen, humanist ideology) only to define itself against it. Indeed, its meaning and purpose derives from the distance it places between itself and ideology. We can go further and say that according to this line of thought, the measurement of a work's distance from ideology is a measurement of its greatness. The greatest form of theater is, then, the critico-realist form, which Althusser in the subtitle to the essay on Bertolazzi and Brecht gives its real name: it is a "materialist theater" the practice of which insofar as it is distinct from ideology disappears into the practice of materialist philosophy (or the materialist practice of philosophy). Thus, if there is contradiction in the realm of art, it is the contradiction between works, between those that reproduce and those that repudiate humanist ideology. Of the former, the great majority of the works produced, there is nothing to be said, their existence need not be explained, their causes are obvious. Of the latter, an extremely small and unrepresentative sample of actually existing works of art (a canon?), one cannot say enough, their power is immense; they transform consciousnesses and lives; they shatter myths and smash the idols to whom we bow down. It is in this sense that the experience of theater, or at least a properly materialist theater, can be "a miracle." In dissociating art into two forms, one devalued and the other idealized, he has reproduced a theory of two arts, two literatures, two cultures: reactionary and progressive (bourgeois and proletarian?), and idealist and materialist. The particular trajectory of this dissociation deprives art of any material existence: in one case it lapses into ideology and in the other it disappears into the practice of philosophy, that practice in which the future of theater lies (according to a passage from Brecht cited by Althusser). It is here that the essay on Brecht and Marx falters and trails off, its incompleteness less a subjective choice on Althusser's part than the palpable effect of a theory that cannot speak of art without reducing it to something other than itself. Althusser cannot proceed further in this direction.

But this is not the only current to which Althusser entrusts himself. In 1966, *La Nouvelle Critique*, the cultural journal of the French Communist Party, published two letters under the title: "Deux lettres sur la connaissance de l'art" (Two letters on the knowledge of art). The first was a kind of open letter to Althusser by a young professor of French literature, André Daspre; the second, Althusser's response to Daspre's questions. Daspre had read Althusser's "Marxism and Humanism" (first published in 1964) and worried that Althusser in his discussion of ideology had ignored or even implicitly rejected the notion that art not only has a specific existence irreducible to ideology, but can convey to us a certain knowledge of ideology and in that sense function as a critique. He appears thus to have identified the strain in Althusser's conception of art discussed above: Althusser's reduction of most works of art to pure ideology, which in "Marxism and Humanism" reinforces rather than modifies the imaginary relation of men to their real conditions of existence, the myths, images and concepts that they take for reality. We might expect Althusser, who is at pains to assure Daspre that he does not regard all art as reducible to ideology, to reprise his statements on Cremonini, Bertolazzi and Brecht and argue that at least the greatest works of art carry out a profound subversion of ideology. Instead, he departs from the alternatives he has prescribed for art (apology or critique) to open a new way for thought.

He begins by saying that he does "not rank true art [*l'art véritable*] among the ideologies." A few sentences later he specifies that what he is about to say in regard to art applies only to "authentic art, not works of an average or mediocre level" (Althusser 1971, 222). Although Althusser thus begins by distinguishing between true and false, authentic and inauthentic art, he abruptly abandons the positions taken in the earlier essays, calling into question the distinctions he has just invoked. It is striking to see the extent to which his approach to the question of art and ideology has suddenly become far more cautious than had been the case in the earlier essays, indicating a rethinking of the positions he had taken: "the problem of the relations between art and ideology is a very complicated and difficult one" (ibid., 221). Rather than directly discuss the precise nature of the complexities and difficulties proper to this relation, or rather proper to any attempt rigorously to understand this relation, Althusser refers Daspre to a recently published essay by his student Pierre Macherey ("Lenin, Critic of Tolstoy") and announces the publication in the near future of "important studies" on which he and his students are working. (In fact, Macherey's *Pour une théorie de la production littéraire* appeared later that same year in Althusser's series with the publisher Maspero.) He then changes direction, introducing a new question, that of the relation between art and knowledge. The absence or omission of what one might expect, a discussion of the relation between art and ideology, especially now that Althusser has declared it a problem essential to any scientific apprehension of literature, is significant.

A review of Macherey's essay suggests a salient reason for such an omission: Macherey's arguments are incompatible with many of Althusser's previous statements. While he has taken certain concepts and terms from Althusser (and has thus appeared to many readers to have simply extended or continued Althusser's theoretical approach), he has in fact given them a new and different meaning. Even in this early essay (and he would develop these ideas much further in *A Theory of Literary Production*), the distinction between great works of art that subvert and mediocre works that faithfully reproduce given ideologies is called radically into question. Such distinctions are made to seem indices of a failure of critical comprehension rather than objective properties of the text. Macherey, who examines Lenin's commentary on Tolstoy very carefully, appropriates the idea that literature is the mirror of its time, insisting that such a notion establishes once and for all the necessary relation of any work of art (and certainly not simply those reputed to be great) to history. All works of art are thus historical and in this relation resides the principle of their intelligibility: all, whatever the quality attributed to them at a particular time, are equally "mirrors" of historical reality. Further, Macherey, quite in contrast to Althusser, rejects any notion of an artist's "talent" or even skill, insisting that one must begin to consider the activity of the artist as a kind of "labor" (*travail*), a term that compels us to account for the labor process as well as for the materials of labor, neither of which can be said to be created or even controlled in any important sense by the artist.

Paradoxically, these notions suggest that faithfully and exactly to reproduce an ideology would itself require greater skill and power than any artist could hope to possess; it would require nothing less than the ability completely to transcend the contradictions and conflicts of one's historical epoch. Instead, Macherey attributes the decentering activity that Althusser reserves for the great works to all art. Speaking specifically about literature (but, of literature as such, not simply certain texts), Macherey argues that it can be called a mirror only in the sense that it is understood as a broken mirror that dismembers what it reflects, separating what is understood commonly as coherent and unified. No matter how coherent its form, it breaks apart what it reflects. The conclusion of Macherey's essay is that the work "projects its thin surface on to the world and on to history. It traverses them, splitting them apart. Following it, in its wake, images arise" (Macherey 1978, 100).

Does this then mean that Macherey, as so many of his critics have charged, attributes to all literary texts the power of subversion and destruction that Althusser ascribed only to a select few? The answer is No: not only has Macherey shifted the discussion from great works of art, in this case, literature, to literature as a whole, but he displaced the discussion of the effects of art from the realm of the directly political (it will impel spectators into action) to the realm of knowledge. The importance of art for Marx, Engels and Lenin is not its agitational or subversive power but its potential contribution to historical knowledge. Nothing about the work itself guarantees that it will so contribute to a knowledge of history (Macherey will say that the work is silent: it says nothing to us and it is we who will speak about it); its contribution to this knowledge remains contingent upon our developing the capacity to produce knowledge about what we now recognize that we only provisionally call art, drama or literature, as well as the capacity to theorize its relation to knowledge.

It is at this point that Althusser's discussion resumes, presupposing Macherey's recasting of his earlier arguments. Art is not knowledge (*connaissance*), or rather, to employ Althusser's formulation, art does not "give us a knowledge in the strict sense" and cannot "replace" knowledge; it does, however, "allow us to see," "allow us to perceive," even "allow us to feel" not reality, of course, but the ideology through which we live our reality (Althusser 1971, 222). The novels of Balzac, for example, allow us to see and feel ideology as ideology, and no longer as reality; in this sense they offer that ideology up for knowledge, although a knowledge which they themselves cannot produce. They exhibit ideology as a system of "conclusions without premises": only scientific knowledge can inquire into and determine the premises that produced these conclusions and the causes that determined the effects the novels allow us to see (ibid., 224).

What is remarkable about these arguments is the degree to which they represent a retreat on Althusser's part from the notion incarnate in the image of *El Nost Milan*, shattering from a distance the fragile glass of the dominant ideology, pursuing itself through him, moving him to feel, to think, to write, to act. The intervention of Macherey was clearly decisive: it has brought about a very sober rethinking of the positions expressed in the essays from the first half of the decade. No longer will even the greatest works of art bring about that miraculous transformation of spectators and readers that would lead us not simply to interpret the world but to change it. In fact, what is surprising is not that at best works of art offer us a kind of raw material for knowledge, it is that the utility even of this material depends upon the adequacy of our theory. And our theory is as yet inadequate: as Althusser frankly admits, we lack the means to "produce a knowledge of art." We do not yet possess "an adequate (scientific) knowledge of the processes which produce the 'aesthetic effect' of the work of art" (ibid., 225). He will caution us even further. Some have confused the recognition that a theoretical apparatus permitting a knowledge of art is necessary with that theoretical apparatus itself, laboring under the illusion that we already possess the theoretical means to produce an adequate knowledge of art and thus need only to begin: "The recognition (even the political recognition) of the existence and importance of art does not constitute a knowledge of art" (ibid., 225). The concepts that arise "spontaneously" to guide the way we think about art (Althusser cites the example of the notion of "aesthetic creation" from Daspre's letter) must be "abandoned" (ibid., 225). Such concepts are not spontaneous at all, but expressions of the ideology of art in relation to which any body of genuinely scientific concepts must mark a rupture and a break.

Does Althusser install himself on the far side of the break with aesthetic ideology to speak as the arbiter of science? On the contrary: he not only admits, but insists on the fact that no such knowledge exists and that we do not even yet possess the means to achieve it. What is now necessary is "slow and arduous work"; we must "spend a long time and pay the greatest attention" to "the basic principles of Marxism" and not be in a hurry to "move on to something else, for if we move on too quickly to 'something else' we shall arrive not at a knowledge of art, but at an ideology of art" (ibid., 227). These words apply and must be applied as much to Althusser's writings on art (including the beginning of the letter itself with its highly "ideological" distinction between great and mediocre works of art) as to anything Daspre says in his short letter. The time has come to set aside questions like "What is art?" or "Why Theater?" (let alone the question of what makes some works of art "great") and ask instead what concepts, themes and myths govern the way we think about art, and further, what is the history and function of the concept "art" (or literature or theater). Althusser is on his way.

Paradoxically, the text that most comprehensively, and with great precision, began systematically to identify and critically examine the concepts that govern our experience of and reflection on art and literature is Althusser's introduction to the collective work *Reading Capital*: "From *Capital* to Marx's Philosophy," a text that does not nominally concern art or literature at all. In a very important sense, however, his arguments work to call radically into question many of the assumptions that guided Althusser's reflections on art; they subject to careful scrutiny the concepts that he elsewhere accepts as givens, beginning with those that seem least open to question. At the outset, he seeks to dispel any idea that *Reading Capital*, although the complete text comes to more than 600 pages, can provide anything other than the "beginnings of a reading." "We have all read, we all read" Marx's text; as an analysis of capitalism from the perspective of labor (the only perspective from which it can be grasped as a whole, according to Marx) its concepts, the phenomena it describes and attempts to explain (e.g., commodities and money – that is, the simple, apparently obvious fact of exchange, namely that the text of the Holy Bible can have a value that is equivalent to that of a sturdy pair of scissors) surround us in our daily lives, where we read them and read about them constantly. But beyond the tyranny of the obvious, which is obvious because it cannot or must not be explained, there exist a host of "philosophers, economists and politicians" whose role is to reaffirm or sanctify the obvious and to erect whole "sciences" on the basis of their truth. Of course, there have been those, the political leaders and theoreticians of the workers' movement, who, against the tyranny of the obvious, especially against the obviousness of the fact that employee and employer meet as equals in the marketplace where they freely enter into a mutually beneficial contractual relation, have in effect "read [Capital] for us, whether well or badly" (Althusser 1975, 3).

Beyond all the obstacles and aids that line the path to *Capital* it is instructive to note Althusser's proposed protocol for reading the text when and if "one day" (ibid., 4) he and his companions reach it: "it is necessary one day to read *Capital* to the letter. To read the text itself in its entirety, all four volumes line by line . . . it is necessary to read *Capital* not only in translation, but . . . in the German original" (ibid., 4). This decisive statement has often been overlooked: previous readers have extracted from Marx's text a set of arguments or meanings, or at least claim to have done so. In fact, their commentaries without exception have failed fundamentally to grasp the text as it is in its literal existence; they have failed to read the German text line by line, to the letter, to determine exactly and fully what it says. In a very real sense, *Capital* is an unexplored and uncharted territory. Each of the contributors to the collective reading initiated by Althusser has thus "cut [*taillé*] his own oblique path through the immense forest of this Book," an "adventure" with both its "risks" and its "advantages" (ibid., 14). If a text that has elicited hundreds of commentaries, attacks and defenses has remained unexplored, if carefully to trace the succession of its words, sentences, paragraphs and chapters is to bring to light a previously unknown reality, even if only the reality of a text, what are we to think about literary texts? They too, even the most famous among them, phrases from which are on everyone's lips and whose meaning is well established, have yet to be confronted in their literal, material existence. Charting the surface of these texts, however tedious and "scholastic" an exercise it may seem, is as likely to produce surprises as the charting of the surface of a distant planet.

All of this means that before Althusser can begin to read the readers reading *Capital* in order then to read it himself to the letter, he must pose the following, apparently simple but in fact very complicated, question: "What is it to read?" (ibid., 15). This extraordinary text begins with the assertion that before we begin to read Marx, which necessarily means before we begin to read those who have read Marx for us and to us, we must consider the problem of what it is to read: What do we do when we read and what is the nature of the object that the act of reading presupposes? Such work is not to be carried out in a vacuum, reasoning from first principles; on the contrary it necessarily takes a historical form: What concepts govern the way we think about reading? What other models of reading have existed? What are the social functions of the models of reading? Further, what other acts and practices apparently so fundamental as to be unquestionable are tied to and presupposed by the concept of reading:

> As paradoxical as it may seem, I venture to suggest that our age threatens one day to appear in the history of human culture as marked by the most dramatic and difficult trial of all, the discovery of and training in the meaning of the" simplest" acts of existence: seeing, listening, speaking, reading– the acts which relate men to their works and to those works thrown in their faces, their "absences of works" [*leur "absences d'oeuvres"*]. (Ibid., 15)

Few, if any, of the many commentators on and critics of *Reading Capital* have taken note of this crucial passage. In particular, the phrase "absences of works," so awkward in English, merits some discussion; it bears directly on Althusser's theory of reading. Althusser took this phrase from the preface to the first edition of Foucault's *Madness and Civilization* (1961),[11] a work that Althusser lectured on and of which he was particularly fond. It is the phrase that for Foucault answers the question "What is then the most general but most concrete form of madness that allows it to escape the grasp of knowledge (*savoir*)?" It is that which in history is silence and which can be spoken of only with words such as "the void, the fleeting, nothingness." It is that absence of work (*oeuvre*) upon which the work of history is founded. If history is intelligible because it is the work of human hands and human minds, whose meaning it embodies, it is doubled by the unintelligible, acts without meaning and speech without significance and thus bodily movements that are nevertheless not acts or works, utterances that are not language, the necessary presence of non-sense to meaning. What can and cannot be read?

Which texts possess or embody meaning and which do not? What in texts has or does not have meaning? In what way is nonsense constitutive of the sense we may derive from texts? These are the questions that Foucault's preface provoked for Althusser.

The question "What is it to read?" then, cannot be answered, from Althusser's point of view, by reducing it to its simplest elements, a reader, a text, etc. and reconstructing, as if in a vacuum, a logical "account" of reading, but by determining the assumptions that govern reading as it is and has been practiced. Althusser argues that both the way we think about and the way we actually practice reading is dominated by a fundamentally "religious model" of knowledge, a model according to which the world is a book (an *oeuvre* in Foucault's sense) whose essence or meaning can be "read" in its appearance. The Spirit inhabits in person "this bread, this body, this face, and this man" the particularity and substantiality of which are dissolved by the act of reading to allow them to reveal the truth that they contain (ibid., 16). The world of nature is a world of appearance, of surface whose meaning lies hidden within it: in the essence beneath appearance, the unity beneath diversity. Knowledge, according to this model, is not the vision that sees, but the reading that deciphers the signs that both express and conceal truth. The religious model of knowledge, according to Althusser, is in no way restricted to theologians: it governs the work of Hegel and even of the young Marx.

But Althusser seems to have moved away from the specificity of reading: How do these philosophical notions affect the way we read texts? How, if at all, have they prevented us from grasping texts in their literal, material existence, as they are, to the letter, line by line and page by page? Here, Althusser takes what he would later call a "detour" in his exposition of Marx. In order to understand the model that, without our understanding either its power or scope, has governed not only our reading of Marx's texts but all texts, he will turn to "the first man ever to have posed the problem of reading, and in consequence, of writing": the seventeenth-century philosopher Spinoza. In *Reading Capital* and elsewhere, Althusser reserves his highest praise for a philosopher still seldom read in the English-speaking world: "Spinoza's philosophy introduced an unprecedented theoretical revolution in the history of philosophy, probably the greatest revolution of all time, insofar as we can regard Spinoza as Marx's only direct ancestor, from a philosophical standpoint" (ibid., 102).

What amounts to Althusser's Spinozist reading of Marx, allows us to understand that Marx's ability "to break with the religious myth of reading" derived from his "rupture with the Hegelian conception of the whole as a spiritual totality, to be precise, as an *expressive* totality."

> It is no accident that when we turn the thin sheet of the theory of reading, we discover beneath it a theory of expression and that we discover this theory of the expressive totality (in which each part is *pars totalis* immediately expressing the whole that it inhabits in person) to be the theory which, in Hegel, for the last time and on the terrain of history itself assembled all the complementary religious myths of the voice (the Logos) speaking in the sequences of a discourse; of the Truth that inhabits its Scripture. (Ibid., 17)

If the Bible becomes the model of all texts and the forms of Biblical interpretation the set of all possible practices of reading, no work could better enable us to break from these myths than Spinoza's *Tractatus Theologico-Politicus*, first published in 1670. Nearly half of Spinoza's text is devoted to a critique of extant notions of the interpretation of Scripture. His arguments proved so incendiary in his own time that he felt compelled to publish the work anonymously, even taking care to conceal the publisher and place of publication. Althusser was fascinated both by Spinoza's work, whose major texts he read again and again over a period of decades,[12] and by its "effects" as he put it, the "terror" it inspired in the theologians and philosophers of his time. What do we find in Spinoza that justifies Althusser's assertion that Spinoza delivered "the greatest lesson in heresy that the world has ever seen," and how does this heresy inform Althusser's own critique of reading?

Spinoza begins his exposition of the proper method of scriptural interpretation with an assertion echoes of which can be seen throughout the opening pages of *Reading Capital*: "I hold that the method of interpreting scripture is no different from the method of interpreting nature." The concept of nature had changed dramatically in Spinoza's century. Once nature was a mere expression of its creator, a veil of appearance that concealed the true essences and ends of all things. We understand the created world only when we pass beyond it or transcend it to find its meaning and purpose. With the revolutions in physics and astronomy associated with Copernicus and Galileo, teleology and transcendence were discredited: matter moved perpetually without origin or purpose but according to immutable laws. The ecclesiastical authorities, of course, did not take kindly to these new theories: Galileo's fate (there was nothing accidental about Althusser's admiration for Brecht's *Galileo*) showed what the practitioners of the new sciences of nature could expect. Today we are more enlightened; such views trouble no one. It remains difficult, however, to see in what way the interpretation of Scripture (let alone, writing in general) can be regarded as "no different than" the interpretation of nature.

Spinoza, who as a Jew had been trained both in Biblical Hebrew and in some of the most important Biblical commentaries and who after his excommunication from the Jewish community had an opportunity to read widely in Christian commentary, noted that, as in the theological view of nature as a mere expression of a truth beyond it, interpreters regarded Scripture as a conduit to a deeper truth, a mere "pretext," as Spinoza put it. The text was a covering, at most a series of clues to the meaning hidden within. Its narratives were not primarily statements of fact (although its literal truth could not be doubted: from Creation to the great Kingdoms) but rather figurations and personifications of the truth that surpasses our understanding. As such, there could be nothing superfluous or inconsistent in Scripture; what appeared so was, by that very fact, the sign of a deeper mystery, a meaning that eluded us. Such points served precisely to goad us on in our never ending quest to demonstrate the perfection of Scripture. The greatest interpreters, men like Rashi, could even divine meaning in the shape of the letters that made up the text.[13] To read Scripture, then, was to show that the apparent disorder of the surface of the text was nothing more than a cover, a veil cast over the truth that it was forbidden directly to see or to say. The more adequate the interpretation the more it could demonstrate the perfection of the text by showing that not a single element, not even the graphic, could fail to have significance. Althusser refers to a similar concept with his phrase "expressive totality": in it, no element, no phenomenon, however apparently trivial or meaningless, can fail to express the spirit of the whole. According to such a conception, to read is an operation of reduction; we reduce the disorder and insignificance of the surface to the ordered meaning of the textual depth.

To treat Scripture as nature, for Spinoza, meant rejecting such an interpretive tradition in its entirety. It meant regarding Scripture as surface without depth, not as appearance concealing a deeper truth hidden to all but the initiated, but as appearance without any concealed essence, except the essence "lyingly added" (to borrow Nietzsche's phrase) by those who have a stake in impeding knowledge and cultivating superstition. Just as theologians exhort us to look beyond this world for its truth, a gesture that devalues it as a necessarily degraded expression of something greater, so they deny or negate Scripture as it actually is in order to impel us to look "within," that is, outside of it for its true meaning and perfection. Spinoza will proceed even further to establish the motive for this disregard of the text as it is: to examine the text as a material artifact composed of elements is to discover that far from exhibiting the perfection that one would expect of the Word of God – the Logos, which inspires and breathes life into what would otherwise be only a collection of dead letters – Scripture is a composite, fabricated at a later age out of contradictory, incomplete and diverse materials. The task of interpretation, which treats Scripture, according to Spinoza, as a "pretext" rather than a text, is to negate or refuse it in its actual existence by claiming to have found within it an order, coherence and homogeneity of meaning and style which, in fact, has been imposed or projected upon Scripture. Spinoza proposes (and this is undoubtedly his "revolution") to take Scripture as it is, its gaps, lacunae, inconsistencies and outright contradictions of doctrine and narrative, as irreducible. From these, its real characteristics, we can begin to explain Scripture as a historical artifact. To look beyond them or to explain them away with hermeneutic procedures would be to overlook that which is to be explained, condemning us to a state of perpetual ignorance.

Armed with a knowledge of Spinoza, Althusser proceeds to read Marx, or more precisely to read Marx reading his predecessors, especially Adam Smith and David Ricardo, by drawing a line of demarcation in Marx's text that makes visible the coexistence of two distinct practices of reading. The first practice of reading looks beyond Smith's text, comparing it to a pre-given reality which it in part sees and in part doesn't see. The conflicts proper to Smith, then, are not internal to his work, but exist in the discrepancy between the text and the reality it attempts, but fails fully, to reflect. Smith according to this first reading has overlooked a crucial part of economic reality. In a certain sense, for Althusser, this is not a true reading at all, in that it doesn't confront the complexity of Smith's text.

Coexisting alongside this first reading that Marx undertakes is a second, genuine, reading that does not find the truth that eluded

Smith outside of his work, in the facts that escaped him, the phenomena that he failed to see or saw only indistinctly. If one can retain the metaphor of vision, and Althusser believes that we can, in order to explain Marx's "protocol of reading," it is only by complicating it in the following way:

> what classical political economy does not see is not what it does not see, it is what it sees; it is not what it lacks, on the contrary it is what it does not lack; it is not what it misses, on the contrary it is what it does not miss. The oversight, then, is not to see what one sees, the oversight no longer concerns the object, but the sight itself. (Ibid., 21)

Marx thus, according to Althusser, has restored the contradiction to Smith's text, showing that the text does not see all that it does; it exhibits irreducibly contradictory economic theories without registering or attempting to resolve this contradiction. How can the text not see what it does? How can it exhibit but not acknowledge what it exhibits? Here Althusser turns to psychoanalysis for the concepts with which to theorize the unrecognized conflicts that appear on the surface of the text. Certain elements are excluded, repressed, split off, denied even as they are stated. They are those things the text cannot help but say, but which nevertheless so disturb the meaning it wishes to project that they become subject to a kind of isolation, an inner darkness of exclusion, that renders them invisible even in their visibility, surrounding them with an absence, the absence of the connection to what the text wants to say and means to say. In a certain sense the entire text is constructed around the need to deny, to make invisible that which it makes visible by diverting our attention from it. Althusser calls this analysis of a text's defenses and conflicts a "symptomatic reading"; it presupposes the coexistence of two texts, one of which becomes visible only when we note the lapses and gaps that normally function to make certain parts of the text illegible.

Macherey's intervention

Interestingly, it was not Althusser himself in his own writings who successfully developed his observations on reading from his introduction to *Reading Capital* into a coherent discussion of literature. The task, instead, was assigned to Pierre Macherey, according to the rough division of labor agreed to by Althusser and his "jeunes chiens" in the elaboration of their collective project. While Macherey gave a presentation at the seminar on Capital (1964–5), a written version of which was published in the first edition of *Reading Capital* under the title "A propos du processus d'exposition du 'Capital' (Le travail des concepts)," his was the shortest of the six contributions to the volume. The bulk of his effort went to his study of literary production, as he then called it, the fruits of which were published in 1966 as *Pour une théorie de la production littéraire*. The title of the English translation of the work omits the first word of the original French: "*Pour*." The omission itself is significant: it is perhaps symptomatic of what remained stubbornly invisible and unreadable to Macherey's erstwhile British interpreters, who, against the words of the text itself, took it as providing the long sought-after Marxist Theory of Literature. Macherey's text sought precisely to identify and dismantle the major obstacles to a theory of literary production in order to make such a theory possible, rather than immediately to supply a theory which could only be the result of an extended period of experimentation and evaluation. Instead, after removing the obstacles to a theory of literary production, he undertakes an experiment, a reading of Jules Verne, that may contribute to but does not itself follow from the construction of a theory. It is important for any understanding of the "Althusserian" approach to literature to appreciate the theoretical prudence or caution of Macherey's endeavor, his sense as he later put it, that to be able to pose a question does not mean that we are able yet to answer it.

Macherey's text illustrates quite nicely Althusser's assertion that Spinoza was the first man to develop a theory of reading: it is Spinozist from beginning to end. Macherey, who was engaged in a *Maitrise* (similar to a Master's Thesis) on Spinoza when he began to work with Althusser while a student at the École Normale Supérieure and who has since become one of the world's foremost Spinoza scholars (having published seven books on Spinoza), organizes his examination of all previous approaches to literary criticism around the hypothesis that criticism is a succession of forms of denial or refusal of the materiality of literary works and of the process by which they are produced. He begins by noting that the term "criticism" itself denotes two irreducibly different activities. On the one hand, the attempt not to know, but to judge a literary work: Is it good or bad, great or merely important? Is Shakespeare greater than Toni

Morrison? Is Chaucer his equal? Admittedly such judgments require great finesse: several centuries ago critics derived rules from Aristotle and applied them without prejudice to the texts whose claims to greatness they sought to adjudicate (Shakespeare did not fare well in their court). Such criteria were eventually dismissed as too rigid, condemning as inferior works that everyone knew (without exactly knowing how they knew) were in fact great. Later, of course, other criteria in increasingly rapid succession supplanted their Aristotelian unities. Works were judged according to their thematic content: did they depict the noble suffering of the solitary individual, the famous human condition, or did they depict the forces of progress in their triumphant struggle against injustice and immorality? They might also be judged by the degree of formal coherence they manifested, irrespective of their content, or the degree to which their parts contributed to the effect of the whole. Discredited, unable to account for the "value" of works that commonly appear in university courses, the jurisdiction of such approaches was called into question. Criticism has increasingly tended to become identified with the component that always irreducibly accompanied and coexisted with the practice of judgment: the attempt to analyze or interpret, to understand the literary work. But why does Macherey insist that these activities, which (although to a lesser extent today than in times past) are often thought to accompany and imply each other, are in fact irreducibly separate?

The most primitive form of criticism, according to Macherey, is that which treats literature as an object of consumption and which sees as its primary task the instruction of the reader in the best techniques for enjoying or "appreciating" the object that is given to them. Not only does this form of criticism accept its object as a given, thereby falling into the most naive kind of empiricism, but it most often endows the work that it appreciates with a mysterious quality. Works are explained by reference to the "genius" of their authors, just as their most important qualities are, from the standpoint of consumption, indefinable. We must depend, as in Hume's famous essay, on the delicacy of the critic's palate; he who is most capable of discriminating among the indefinable shades of literary greatness.[14] Surely, it will be objected, such "technicians of taste," to use Macherey's phrase, have dwindled to extinction in academia. One need only consult Harold Bloom's bestseller (and Bloom is a critic who has shown himself, at least in an earlier incarnation, to be capable of more than the "profundities" of his later work). He must read for us, teach us how and what to read, those of us reared in the "Chaotic Age" (his phrase and capitalization) corrupted by television (Bloom informs us that he did not own a television until he was forty) and unable to "read deeply." In his conclusion to this prolix defense (578 pages) of Great Literature against a bewildering array of enemies, he is compelled to move beyond the references to unknowable and incomprehensible greatness (perhaps television has robbed us of the ability to believe or to have faith); great literature is great to the extent that it engages us to acknowledge our "solitude" and "mortality." Of course, those who daily face their solitude and mortality will have no need for literature (except perhaps the consolation it brings) and the fact that they increasingly outnumber those with the luxury of forgetting these truths appears to bode ill for the future of literary studies. Like all luxury goods, however, literature will find its niche even amid the increasing mortality rates and economic abandonment, and Bloom will be there to teach us how best to enjoy it.

The example of Bloom is instructive in another way: it shows the extent to which the critical approach sketched out above is often linked to another critical fallacy, the normative fallacy:

> Behind the critical attitude there is an implicit but decisive affirmation: "it could or ought to be different." Criticism thus has both a positive and a negative aspect: by reference to an ideal norm it destroys that which is, substituting a revised, corrected and consistent version of an initial reality. It does not matter that this elaboration expresses an ideal and a wish; for not only is the possible preferred to the real, but the real itself is depicted as the possible form of a norm, given at the same moment. (Macherey 1978, 15)

Judgment begins, then, with the gesture of refusal: what is important is not what the work is, but rather what it is not. Criticism, according to this model, must refuse the work and look beyond it to the ideal in relation to which it will be judged great, good, fair, poor or bad according to the degree to which it corresponds to this ideal. There is something Platonic here: the norm is the ideal form whose emanations or expression are always less than, or degraded versions of, the form or essence they express. Bloom perfectly illustrates Macherey's argument about "how closely the empiricist and normative fallacies are related" (ibid., 17).

Macherey's work, which, as we shall soon see, is opposed to structuralism in so many ways, is nevertheless allied with it quite successfully against a central concept in literary studies, that of the canon. His choice of the work of Jules Verne, a "minor" author, even an author of children's books, as the object of study is significant. For structuralists one could no more study the "great works" of literature alone than linguistics could afford to study only eloquent statements (or for that matter, any more than biology can afford to study only "advanced" organisms, botany beautiful flowers or physics only the aesthetically rewarding patterns created by plasma). If we seek to understand and to explain how what we now provisionally call "literature" and "literary texts" come into being, or to use Spinoza's language, their causes, we must, as in linguistics, be able to explain every text, the conditions of its existence. Macherey here takes a materialist position: texts in their historical existence are irreducibly real; they cannot be understood as expressions of something which, although posing as more real, is in fact not real at all. We cannot explain that which exists by pointing to the ideal that it should have realized but failed to. Spinoza formulated this position as an epigram whose capacity to shock and provoke has remained undiminished as we enter the twenty-first century: "By reality and perfection I mean the same thing" (Spinoza 1992, *Ethics* II, Definitions, Explication 6).

The invalidation of any normative approach to literature as fundamentally at odds with the project of explaining it, that is, of formulating knowledge about it, is not only a necessary first step in understanding literary texts through their causes; it permits an inquiry into the emergence of literature itself. In particular it allows us to examine the function of the concept of "canon." In one sense, of course, canon formation (the selection of the eternally important works from the dross of all their seemingly numberless companions, and defense of the same) has little to do with knowledge in any rigorous sense, except perhaps the knowledge of the limits of knowledge, that is, of the mysteries of existence (our own or in general, it matters little) that we neither can nor should seek to dispel. One cannot speak of mysteries; it is to be understood that the vague attempts to define what makes great works great are only the merest of approximations; such works are like the God of the Hebrew people who cannot be named or denoted directly, but only alluded to by His attributes. So for Bloom one can never exactly say what makes Shakespeare the center of the canon: when we speak of him, his meaning eludes our words, he has already written more than we can ever think or say. But Macherey's immediate objective had less to do with Bloom's French predecessors than with a settling of accounts with the French Communist Party's residual Stalinism (the effects of which, as we have seen, Althusser did not entirely escape). For canons have not simply functioned as mechanisms for securing the hegemony of the ruling ideas by excluding works that challenge them or their assumptions. The Communist tradition offered its own canon, usually composed of authors excluded from the traditional canons, based on the proletarian or democratic character of the literary work. In fact, the bulk of critical activity carried out under the auspices of Communist parties consisted of denunciations of literary works produced in what was assumed to be the final stages of a dying capitalist culture. Macherey's attack on the normative fallacy reveals that the construction of any canon whatever, progressive or reactionary, an activity that must to a great extent consist of the exclusion and denunciation of a large part of the reality under consideration, remains an obstacle to the historical knowledge upon which any successful social transformation must in part depend.

The notions of a criticism whose primary function is to appreciate or judge, however important they remain outside of academic study, are increasingly irrelevant within it. Bloom's fears of a counter-canon (and it is this that he fears more than a rigorous questioning of the notion of a canon in the service of knowledge – an alternative that doesn't appear to occur to him) from which all the "dead white males" with whose spirits he regularly communicates would be excluded, is nothing more than a fantasy, an inverted image of his own fanaticism. Part of any movement away from the normative fallacy and its noxious ratings systems has been of course a recovery and study of works previously excluded (designated as "minor" or merely "bad"), ignored, or even unknown, an activity that must continue for some time. In fact, most critical approaches to literature attempt to explain rather than judge, and even those that judge employ at least rudimentary forms of analysis. As Macherey points out, however, the renunciation of criticism as judgment in no way ensures an acknowledgment of the text as it is in its material, literal existence; on the contrary, some of the most powerful obstacles that stand in the way of reading present themselves as modes of apprehending the reality and truth of literary works.

For Macherey, what we will provisionally agree to call literature, recognizing that the object we construct at the culmination of our inquiry may no longer correspond to that particular appellation, becomes the "object of a rational study" when we recognize that "the work is therefore determined: it is itself and nothing else" (Macherey 1978, 52). To begin with the second half of the statement, to say that the work is itself and nothing else, means that it is irreducible to something supposedly more real, something prior to itself. This is another way of identifying the material existence of the literary work: it possesses a reality, it is not the shadow of the real, a simulation, an illusion. However, "under the pretext of exorcizing any inclination to reduction, we must not consider the literary work in isolation, as if it constituted by itself a complete reality; it would thus be absolutely separate and we wouldn't be able to understand the reason for its appearance" (ibid., 67). This conception of art (the idea that art transcends or even has nothing to do with politics and history) renders the work inexplicable insofar as art is precisely that which cannot be explained or known, but only felt or appreciated. As Macherey points out, this is a profoundly religious conception of art which assigns it to the order of the miraculous (that which cannot be explained, that which defies and surpasses human understanding), according it the status of a mystery whose origins and existence can never be known.

Macherey must then couple the assertion that the work is determined or caused with the assertion that it possesses a material existence, that it is real, objective and as such irreducible to something more real than itself, as if it were mere phenomena or appearance. The linking of these two propositions is crucial given that they have functioned in the history of criticism as if they were antithetical: either the work is reducible to something else of which it is the expression, representation or reflection (all terms which Macherey cautions are entirely inadequate as currently understood) or it is absolutely free from any determination at all, uncaused, miraculous and therefore inexplicable. To begin, then, with the recognition that to say that the work is determined is insufficient. We must draw a line of demarcation between two opposed ways of thinking about the way a work might be determined: on the one hand, a notion of determination that deprives the work of its reality, that connects it to history only by making it disappear into that which it reflects or expresses; on the other, a notion of determination that explains the work in its material existence, in its irreducibility. The drawing of such a line in turn makes visible the concepts that, most often unawares, have governed our attempts to conceptualize the causes of the work of art.

It is useful to recall Spinoza's assertion that the method of interpreting scripture is the same as that of interpreting nature. This otherwise strange phrase placed in the context of his philosophical project, serves to remind us how much our notion of literary creation depends upon and commingles with a kind of theology. Once, it was thought that nature was the Creation of the Author of all that has been, is now and ever will be, in a moment of genesis, a beginning before which there was nothing. The idea of creation serves two purposes: it offers an "explanation" of the cause of that which is created, and it functions as a hermeneutic principle that allows us to determine the meaning of that which is created. According to this model, the truth of nature is not in it, but outside of it, a truth that it veils, the truth of God's will: the purpose for which he created all creatures great and small, all things terrestrial. The act of knowing is the act of stripping away the veil of appearances to recover the hidden truth.

In a passage from the *Ethics* that profoundly influenced Althusser and echoes of which may be found throughout his work, Spinoza denounced not only the anthropomorphic conception of God as author as a projection upon the infinite of human characteristics, but went on to argue that the human image projected onto the infinite is precisely that, an image, a product of the imagination. At the center of this anthropological/theological circle is the idea of free will: the Human/God conceives or desires and freely acts to realize the conception or fulfill the desire. We imagine this to be the case because individuals "are conscious of their actions and appetites but unaware of the causes by which they are determined to seek something" (Spinoza 1992, *Ethics* IV, Preface). It is at this point in the argument that Spinoza isolates the example of art, and in particular, painting, as a model for such imaginary notions. In what is perhaps the most heretical moment in this very heretical text, Spinoza argues that we must reject the notion that the mind determines the body to act and instead seek to ascertain the extent to which bodies are moved by other bodies, by other physical forces. Spinoza asks us to reconsider the notion that a painting is the product of an intention, a will to act that originates in the immaterial interior of the mind and then causes the hand to move the brush across the canvas.

In a profound sense, Macherey has simply extended Spinoza's argument to the domain of literature. He denounces the notion of author as creator as an anthropology (a theory of human essence or nature) that is itself "merely an impoverished and inverted theology: in the place of the god–man is installed Man, god over himself" (Macherey 1978, 66). The very idea of artistic creation transmits theology into the discussion of human practice; creation is a theoretical compromise that prevents us from theorizing the determination of works of art even as it masquerades as an explanation:

> the various "theories" of creation all ignore the process of making; they omit any account of production. One can create undiminished, so, paradoxically, creation is the release of what is already there, or one is witness to a sudden apparition, and then creation is an irruption, an epiphany, a mystery. In both cases the means of explaining the change have been suppressed; in one, nothing has happened, and in the other, what has happened is inexplicable. All speculation on man as creator is destined to eliminate real knowledge. (Ibid., 68)

In opposition, Macherey will start from Spinoza's provocative thesis and postulate a notion of literary production:

> art is a product, not of man, but of that which produces it (and the producer is not a subject centered in his creation, he is an element in a situation or a system). . . . Before disposing of these works which can only be called theirs by an elaborate evasion, men must produce them, not by the magic of an advent but by the means of a real labor of production. If man creates man, the artist produces works, in determinate conditions, working not on himself but on that thing that escapes him in so many ways and which only belongs to him retroactively. (Ibid., 67–8E)

Thus, even as the writer thinks or imagines that he creates, that he freely chooses how and what he will write, Macherey insists that he has no more mastery or control over what he does than the worker on the assembly line who chooses neither the materials with which he works, nor the processes by which he assembles these materials. To speak of literary production is to address the question of the forms of determination that make the work what it is. Removing the author from the center of the process of production compels us to think historically about the different relations individuals have had with the works and texts that bear their name, the different processes in which they have been inserted (even as they dreamed they were inventing and creating) and the divergent materials they have used in fabricating a work or works.[15] But what Macherey calls the "subjective" form of authorship is accompanied by an "objective," anonymous form that is mistaken for a rejection of the author altogether. Formalist and structuralist approaches to literature, taking language as their model, argued that the individual writer of literature was as inconsequential to the literary text as the individual speaker is in the case of language. Just as linguists began to conceptualize language as a set of elements (e.g., phonemes, morphemes, words, sentences) combined into meaningful units according to a set of rules, a scheme in which the personal qualities of the speaker were irrelevant, so literary scholars could conceive of literary texts as extended utterances composed of pre-given elements according to pre-given rules that individual authors were not free to alter and in most cases of which they were absolutely ignorant. The goal was, then, to identify and enumerate the elements of which literature was composed (the literary equivalent of phonemes and morphemes) and the rules governing their combination into higher units.[16] As Macherey points out, although this approach to literature appears to dispense with the very notion of the author, in fact, it simply displaces the problems posed by the notion of the author to the level of the system as a whole, which becomes a collective, anonymous author. Neither formalism nor structuralism can explain the emergence of the system nor how, out of the set of potential narratives, one rather than another is generated. We are again faced with epiphanies and miracles: God contains all that could be and we are doomed to remain ignorant of his reasons for selecting among infinite possibilities those that he actualizes.

Macherey has thus identified the ways in which, in the guise of explaining the literary work, critics have reduced it to an intention (subjective or objective, individual or collective, psychological or structural) external to it, an origin to which it would be restored. These, however, are not the only ways in which criticism denies the objective existence of the literary text. Even as it renounces the search for its real existence outside of it, criticism may reduce the work to an internal principle, whether a structure or meaning, hidden within it. First, as Macherey ironically remarks, "a criticism with any aspirations to profundity chooses as its purpose the determination of a meaning" (ibid., 75). Such an approach is not content to describe the work, the rhetorical and literary devices proper to it, any more than it would be satisfied with the mere enjoyment of the text. Interpretation seeks that meaning that proves inaccessible on first reading, a meaning that can be recovered only with great care. The concept of interpretation must, then, itself depend on a set of principles that justify and make necessary its activity: "The work encloses a meaning which must be released; the letter of the work is a mask, eloquent and deceptive, which this meaning bears; a knowledge of the work is an ascent to this central unique meaning" (ibid., 76E). Interpretation depends on the notion that the literary work possesses an exterior and an interior, a surface and a depth. The surface is regarded as the site of "deception" or, as Spinoza argues in the case of Biblical interpretation, a mere "pretext": it offers to the uninitiated reader, especially in the case of "great" works which are by their very nature "difficult," a spectacle of disorder the significance of which is difficult to grasp. In steps the critic to "interpret" or translate, to repeat in other words what the text says. The critic's repetition is however, "a strange repetition that says more by saying less: a purifying repetition at the end of which a hidden meaning appears in all its naked truth. The work is only the expression of this meaning an ore which must be smelted to extract its precious content" (ibid., 76E). The act of interpretation thus not only translates, it reduces the work to its meaning. It demonstrates that the apparent diversity of the work is in fact an expression of the unity of meaning that underlies it. The greatest critic is the one who can show that not a metaphor, an image, a character, an incident when viewed correctly fails to embody, to express, the meaning of the whole.

Macherey extends his critique to that approach to literature seemingly most opposed to interpretation: structuralism. Whatever the function of the idea of structure in fields like linguistics or anthropology, in literature it reintroduces the traditional search for an intrinsic meaning or message that the work transmits, but in a coded form that requires the services of a translator. Structuralism, despite its attempts to break from the traditional search for meaning, repeats its fundamental gesture: the work is the simulacrum of its structure. The job of the critic is to reconstitute that hidden essence. The fact that the unity of the work is one of form rather than meaning matters little here: what matters is the idea of the totality, an idea that requires the repression or denial of all that escapes or opposes the work's fictitious unity. This in turn produces a most unstructuralist paradox: unlike the case of language where syntactical structure, for example, accounts for every possible syntactical variant, in literature the structure of each text "is closed upon itself: the structuralist critic would like to be able, in the manner of Leibniz's God, to pass from one structure to the next, declaring the reasons for this universal harmony, though lacking the means for this task" (ibid., 145). At its most coherent, structuralism can only relate the work to a set of ideal possibilities, the set of all possible texts, most of which do not (yet?) exist.

Macherey concludes the first section of *Theory* by declaring that he has sought to "exorcize" the "illusions that have tied literary criticism to ideology," preventing it from producing a genuine knowledge about the object it studies: particularly, the illusions of the unity of the work, the depth of the work, the hidden meaning of the work, the creation of the work. His theoretical activity, however, has not been restricted to a labor of the negative that dismantles the obstacles on the way to knowledge. Indeed, the work of criticizing certain positions can only itself be accomplished by taking another different position. Thus, he must advance a set of working hypotheses to be tested; the effects of these hypotheses will determine whether or not they are correct and productive. He begins with the assertion that "the work does not contain a meaning which it conceals by giving it its finished form (ibid., 78). "The work hides nothing, contains nothing, holds no secret" (ibid 99). "The work has no interior, no exterior or rather its interior is like an exterior on display, shattered" (ibid., 96). The work is, then, a surface without depth, a surface irreducible to anything else internal or external. This irreducibility precisely constitutes the material existence of the work. It does not in any ordinary sense of the term express, represent or reflect something more real. This is a necessary first hypothesis in that it compels us to explain the work as it is without recourse to any reduction. *The work as it is*: "The concealed order of the work is thus less significant than its real determinate disorder (its disarray). The order which it professes is merely an imagined order, projected on to disorder, the fictive resolution of ideological conflicts" (ibid., 155). Thus "the postulated unity of the work which more or less explicitly has always haunted the enterprise of criticism, must now be denounced" (ibid., 78). To regard the work as irreducible is to begin to recover the way in which the work exhibits a multiplicity of meanings, the way that it, unbeknownst to itself, diverges from itself, to produce absolutely conflicting meanings. Its faults, inconsistencies and contradictions, then, are not signs of artistic failure but of the historical necessity that made the work what it is and no other. In this sense (and here we rejoin Althusser in the exploration of the notion of symptomatic reading), to produce a knowledge of the work is to grasp not only what it says but what it does not and cannot say: the absent conjunctions (whether of addition or opposition) between the divergent meanings, that are not hidden even if the silences that separate them render certain of them illegible, the empty spaces (to borrow a phrase from Spinoza[17]) that divide the work from itself, that separate it into a multiplicity. The silences, these empty spaces, are the signs of the work's incompleteness, the signs of its dependence, even in its irreducibility, on history. It is not external to this history but part of it, thrown up and torn asunder by its conflicts. If the work "is fissured unmade in its very making . . . the disorder of the work is related to the disorder of ideology" (ibid., 155).

Rethinking the concept of ideology

Ideology: It is, then, on this concept that the explanatory power of Althusser's and Macherey's theses on art and literature rests. Ideology is a term closely associated with Althusser and one that he used frequently but without examining it in any systematic fashion until after 1968. The most extended treatment of the concept appears in the 1963 essay "Marxism and Humanism" (and which, as we have noted, stimulated the exchange with André Daspre on art).

For the purposes of his discussion of humanism "it is sufficient to know that . . . an ideology is a system (possessing its own logic and rigor) of representations (images, myths, ideas or concepts, depending on the case) endowed with an existence and a historical role in the midst of a given society" (Althusser 1969, 238). He will complete this definition by opposing ideology not to reality or truth but to science: ideology is distinguished from science by virtue of the fact that its "practico-social function" is dominant over its "theoretical or knowledge function" (ibid., 238). In certain respects, Althusser's definition of ideology remains faithful to that advanced by Marx in the famous passages from *The German Ideology* (1846) and the Preface to *The Contribution to the Critique of Political Economy*: ideology is the superstructure that is determined by the economic base or infrastructure, and which it not only reflects but acts to justify: the economic relations in a given society. Thus, in capitalist societies, law, morality, religion, philosophy and even art present, often in subtle forms, the existing economic relations as natural, normal, right and/or (at the extreme) inescapable. In this way, ideology helps persuade us (along with other means of inducement: hunger, poverty and, when all else fails, armed force) to accept them. We learn to respect the property of others (especially when we have none) no matter how great their wealth and how deprived the populace. We learn to obey the law, in the sight of which rich and poor are free and equal. However crude such notions may now appear, they helped transform the way we think about culture: ideas, beliefs, philosophical doctrines do not originate in an intellectual realm far beyond the ignoble strife, nor do we freely accept or reject the ideas we hold. Instead ideas arise from and are held in place by social and economic relations. From this, Marx concluded that criticism was powerless except to the extent it was tied to practical activity, especially practical activity that successfully resisted the exploitation that lies at the heart of every society divided into classes that labor and a class that appropriates the surplus of that labor.

Althusser's notion of ideology, however, also differs in certain respects from that of Marx. In particular, the opposition between science and ideology is no longer cast as an opposition between the true and the false or between reality and appearance. Ideology itself is no longer a form of deception; it is, rather, the set of "representations" whose function is more practical than theoretical, a definition that allows him to say no society can escape ideology (not even a society without exploitation and class domination) and to imply that ideology must be the site of conflict between those sets of ideas that justify and those that challenge the existing economic order. It is that element in which people become conscious of the contradictions of their social conditions and take sides in the conflict. Althusser will go so far as to say that an "imaginary" element is irreducibly united with any apprehension of the real.

The term "imaginary" here, which many commentators have associated with the psychoanalyst Jacques Lacan, probably owes more to Spinoza's definition of the imaginary as the inversion of causes and effects in human life: we imagine we are the origins, causes and masters of our thought, speech and action when in fact we are simply unaware of the causes that have determined us to think, speak and act as we do. And rulers and ruled alike are subject to the imaginary; it is clear that such a definition of ideology excludes any "instrumental" conception of ideology: even if the dominant ideology is the ideology of the dominant class, that class is not free to use that ideology as it sees fit, knowing in its heart of hearts (like Plato, who sought to invent "noble fictions" or religious myths to deceive the many into obeying their betters) that its ideas are false. Ideology is not a matter of belief at all, it is not the ideas that people think they hold and which would then cause them to act in certain ways. Ideology, Althusser argues, is not a matter of consciousness, it is an unconscious structure which determines both how people will think and how they will act (without there being any necessary correspondence between the two), those who resist as well as those who affirm the established order. He calls it the structure of their manner of living their relations to their conditions of existence and structure here (like the term "system" earlier) cannot, if we follow Althusser's arguments to the letter, be reduced to an order but must be thought of as the coexistence of the heterogeneous, the conflictual and the irregular. We may now understand the sense in which ideology constitutes the raw material of the work of literature or art. In representing reality, the work of art cannot help but represent (or re-present) that imaginary element which remains inseparable from the real. In trying to impose form on the heterogeneous forces that make up the real it falls victim to its own imaginary, revealing disorder and contradiction, themselves the effects of inescapable social struggle.

But if the concept of ideology specific to Althusser explained certain properties of the work of art, it failed in one important respect, perhaps the most important respect. If, as Macherey argued, "the work becomes the object of a rational study" at the moment that it is understood to be "itself and nothing else" (Macherey 1978, 52), that it is regarded as "irreducible . . . to what it is not" (ibid., 51), ideology, as defined by Althusser in his 1963 essay, does not permit us to grasp the nature of that irreducibility or materiality. Ideology, let us recall, is a "system of representations" through which people live their relation to the real (Althusser 1969, 238) and later "an expression of the . . . (overdetermined) unity of their real relation and their imaginary relation to their real conditions of existence" (ibid., 240). If ideology were the raw material of the work of art, the latter would then become a representation of a representation, the expression of an expression and thus situated at a certain distance from the real. But what does it mean to say "outside the real," which is only represented or reflected by the work of art. To say that "this representation of what is already itself a representation precisely calls attention to the ideological or imaginary nature of ideology," does not solve the problem. Conceived in this way, the work would be deprived of its substance: it is an ideal, strictly speaking – a false representation of the reality and history which lie outside of it. We would thus value the work only insofar as it functioned as a conduit to a truth outside of it, a ladder that, once it is scaled, can be cast aside. Our ability to conceptualize the irreducibility and materiality of the work is inescapably tied to our ability to theorize the materiality of ideology, the sense in which it is not simply a system of representations (adequate or inadequate) but itself fully real.

Althusser's last major work and in certain ways his most influential represented precisely an attempt to rectify the concept of ideology described in his 1963 essay. Written immediately following the French general strike of 1968, Althusser's essay "Ideology and Ideological State Apparatuses" (1970) constituted, along with such other works from the period as Deleuze and Guattari's *Anti-Oedipus* (1972) and Foucault's *Discipline and Punish* (1975), a meditation on the failure of the revolt to blossom into revolution. They all, in different ways, attempted to come to grips with the central question of Spinoza's *Tractatus Theologico-Politicus*: "what makes men fight as bravely for their servitude as for their salvation" (Spinoza 1991, Preface). Althusser's essay was extracted from a much longer manuscript entitled "De la superstructure," which remained unpublished during Althusser's lifetime.[18] In it, Althusser attempts to explain what he calls "the reproduction of the relations of production," that is, the reproduction of class exploitation, in which one class not itself directly engaged in productive activity appropriates the surplus produced by those who are engaged in productive activity. Earlier theoreticians from Marx on, explained this unremunerated surrender of a part of the fruits of one's labor by recourse to one (or both) of two alternatives: force or persuasion. In slavery, for example, the slave works for the master out of fear of bodily pain or death, not because the slave "believes in" slavery. In capitalist societies, the appropriation of the laborer's surplus is rendered invisible: labor becomes a contractual agreement between equals, between property owners. One, who owns the means of production, buys the labor-power of the other for a specified length of time. No one has to rouse the worker or threaten him with bodily harm to convince him to begin work: he does so of his own accord (although cold and hunger prove excellent stimulants in a free-market economy). In the case of capitalism, the use of force is unnecessary except in exceptional conditions.

Does that mean then that persuasion becomes the primary means of assuring domination? For Althusser, the opposition of force and persuasion or force and consent is based on the opposition of body and mind: violence works upon the body while persuasion is excercised on the mind, which, as we all know, determines the body to act. People consent to their own servitude according to such theories but their consent is "manufactured" by the educational system and the media. If only opposing views could be aired with similar frequency, such consent would surely crumble away. Literature, art and especially, in the contemporary period, cinema would most of the time function to affirm a false consciousness for which class domination and exploitation would be transmuted into a dimension, whether tragic or heroic, of an eternal human condition.

As a good Spinozist Althusser rejected such oppositions as untenable. Against every separation of body and mind, of force and consent, Althusser transformed everything about the concept but its name, depriving it of any but a material existence. Ideology "represents" (he now places the word in quotation marks) not the reality of social relations in a given society, nor even a distorted view of this reality. Instead ideology 'represents" the imaginary relation of individuals to these social relations. Although Althusser retains the terms "representation" and "imaginary," he gives them an entirely different meaning by insisting that ideology (that is, the imaginary representation of individuals' relation to their real conditions of existence) has a material existence. In the ideological imaginary, then, individuals are free and autonomous, each the cause of his actions, for which he alone is responsible. However false we may believe this relation to be as an explanation of human conduct, it is none-the-less real: countless institutions, apparatuses and practices work to produce this free individual, master of himself. The law is not as set of disembodied illusions which may be accepted or rejected at will; the law is a material reality, its concepts, even the morality it claims to uphold, embodied in a system of discipline and punishment. Similarly, the notion of the autonomous individual, fundamentally separate from others, is a fiction insofar as it is posed as the human condition or the state of nature. Nevertheless, this separation is real: as Foucault has demonstrated at great length, time and space are so organized in capitalist societies as to separate and individualize, replacing collectivities with dissociated individuals. This is the meaning of Althusser's final and most famous thesis concerning ideology: ideology interpellates individuals as subjects.

It is not unthinkable that Althusser borrowed the term "interpellation" from Beckett's *Molloy* in a passage that, if not the source of his theoretical postulate, may serve as a salient illustration of it. Molloy, Beckett's narrator, can walk only with the aid of a crutch and then only with great difficulty. In spite of his handicap, he travels by bicycle (providing Beckett with an ample fund of slapstick imagery). As he approaches a certain town, he dismounts in compliance with town regulations. With great difficulty, he tells us, he manages to advance

> "on my crutches pushing my bicycle at the same time. . . . But a little further on I heard myself hailed (*interpellé*). I raised my head and saw a policeman. . . . What are you doing there, he said. Resting I said. Will you answer my question, he cried. . . . I won't reconstruct the conversation in all its meanderings. It ended in my understanding that my way of resting, my attitude when at rest, astride the bicycle, my arms on my handlebars, my head on my arms, was a violation of I don't know what, public order, public decency. Modestly, I pointed to my crutches and ventured one or two noises regarding my infirmity, which obliged me to rest as I could, rather than as I should. But there are not two laws, that was the next thing I thought I understood, one for the healthy, another for the sick, but one only to which all must bow, rich and poor, young and old, happy and sad. He was eloquent. I pointed out that I was not sad. That was a mistake. Your papers, he said. (Beckett, *Three Novels*, 1976, 20)

Molloy is interpellated and finally subject to identification by the law, which endows him with absolutely free will, demands of him what he cannot do and then declares him a criminal for failing to do it. It is only after he is determined to have intentionally broken the law that he is asked to identify himself by producing his papers. Equality before the law not only ceases to be the expression of a fundamental human commonality, it becomes the principle of differentiation that exonerates the powerful and declares those without jobs or homes voluntary criminals; masters of their own fate, they are judged guilty and punished accordingly. We might think of the tragic–comic spectacle of our own Molloys: those vagrants who are prohibited by law from sleeping on either public or private property.

Althusser will go so far as to say at this point in his essay that ideas and beliefs disappear into practices, consciousness into physical action or behavior. Even religious ideas have no existence apart from institutions, rituals and bodily movements: if individuals do not behave according to what they think they believe, it is because they do not know what they believe. But if ideas, beliefs, even subjectivity itself only exist in material form, incarnate in practices, how then are we to conceive of literature? Does not literature express thoughts, beliefs, images, all of which originate in the mind before they are given outward expression? Here, Althusser follows Derrida in arguing that there is no interiority, no realm outside of and prior to the materiality of discourse. No matter how far back we trace an idea, we find only words; behind the signifier only another signifier. There is no spirit behind the letter. As Lacan put it, the letter "produces all the effects of truth in man without involving the spirit at all" (Lacan 1977, 158).

The literary text is a material artifact produced from certain materials under certain historically determinate circumstances and bears in its very form, its letter, the struggles, the clashes, the warfare that traverse the social realm. The fact that the work, irreducible to a meaning concealed within it and containing not the slightest trace of a spirit that would confer upon it, once and for all, its truth, is finally revealed to be disordered, contradictory and incomplete, serves not simply as the beginning of an explanation of its production, but also, and perhaps just as importantly, serves to pose the question of its reproduction. As Macherey has argued in a recent "rectification" of his earlier work, to consider literature solely from the point of view of production leads to "insurmountable contradictions" (Macherey 1998, 42). To posit the work as "belonging" to the moment of its historical emergence is "to condemn it to become outdated and no longer to exist except in the form of a relic in the absence of the social content in relation to which it was produced" (ibid., 43). A knowledge of literature cannot consist solely of the knowledge of its appearance, as if it will be forever what it was at that originary moment, all subsequent readings of it judged adequate or inadequate in relation to this truth, this identity. The very materiality of works allows them to persist beyond "their" moment and the form of this materiality, its irreducible diversity and incompleteness, can only lead to the conclusion that works are not at all

> produced as such, but begin to exist only from the moment that they are "reproduced," this reproduction having the effect of dividing them within themselves, by tracing the thin line of their discourse in

> such a way as to make an entire space of gap and play appear in it, into which seeps the indefinite possibility of variations. Instead of being produced only once in its place and time, the work thus has realities in the plural only in this mirroring which constitutes it at the same time it disperses it. (Ibid., 47)

Not only is the work a palimpsest, written over other texts to which it "implicitly or explicitly refers" (ibid., 49), but the work itself is constantly reinscribed in other works, perpetually transformed by its encounter with what it is not, not merely other literary texts, but discourses of all kinds, and the practices and institutions in which these discourses are embedded. As we shall see, even texts as often studied as Defoe's *Robinson Crusoe* and Conrad's *Heart of Darkness* are not finished monuments waiting only to be described. On the contrary, they can only be described as works at the cost of a certain distortion: they are perhaps better understood as open processes, transformed by the movement of history itself.

Althusser would go no further in this direction: by 1970 the darkness was already falling on him, the darkness of terrible suffering and tragedy. Althusser would write to Macherey in 1973 that he was no longer capable of "writing new books on new things" (ibid., 12). He had already been borne away by the impassible rivers and would explore no more. He was left to sail on darkened waters, reflected stars scattering around his fragile craft like so many resplendent splinters of shattered glass.

Notes

1. Althusser's *Journal de captivité: Stalag XA, 1940–1945* (Paris: Stock/IMEC, 1992) records not only one of the most difficult periods in a very difficult life, the five years he spent as a prisoner of war in a German prison camp, but also perhaps the most important period of transition. Althusser entered the war at the age of twenty-one, a devout Catholic and a monarchist; he left it a communist in all but party affiliation (by no means an unusual trajectory for his generation). Although he was initially assigned to hard labor, Althusser's mental and physical fragility became obvious and he was reassigned to the camp infirmary and later to the job of assistant to the elected spokesman for the French prisoners. These highly coveted jobs gave him ample time and opportunity for reading. His journal suggests that literature became a kind of

escape for him. In any case, he read widely mainly in French and German literature, as well as Greek tragedy; his readings included Goethe, Holderlin, Nietzsche and Rilke; Montaigne, Pascal, La Bruyère, La Rochefoucauld, Balzac, Stendhal, Claudel, Péguy, Mauriac, Gide; Euripides and Sophocles; D. H. Lawrence and T. S. Eliot. Yann Moulier Boutang in his valuable commentary on the text suggests that Althusser's mature writing style took shape during this period, a consequence of a close reading of French authors (Althusser would copy selected passages in his journal) and translation of German authors. As has been the case with other prisoners, Althusser's study of literature during this five-year period was neither casual nor haphazard: it was an intense engagement with powerful texts of poetry, drama and prose that decisively altered his writing and thought. In one of the darkest moments of his life, he found solace in Goethe and Nietzsche, in Pascal and Péguy. This partially explains how Althusser who was drafted shortly before he was to begin his university study at the École Normale Supérieure, and only began his course of study upon his return in 1945, was able, after a mere two years at the École, to write an extraordinary thesis on Hegel (one that Merleau-Ponty sought unsuccessfully to persuade him to publish). The years in the prison camp had been, as his biographer suggests, the equivalent of university study for him.

2. Hélène Legotien, a sociologist and Althusser's companion for many years whom he married in 1972. During a delusional state, he strangled her in 1980, an act he explores in detail in his autobiography, *The Future Lasts Forever.* Bernard Dort was an influential critic and theoretician of theater.
3. In 1845, Marx settled accounts with the materialist humanism of philosopher Ludwig Feuerbach with a set of eleven theses on the shortcomings of Feuerbach's thought. The eleventh and final thesis, to which Madonia refers represented to many Marxists an abandonment of philosophy; for Althusser it was, rather, a call for a new practice of philosophy, for a philosophy that recognized its practical existence: "The philosophers have only interpreted the world in various ways; the point is to change it" (Marx 1998, 123).
4. See Althusser, *Écrits philosophiques et politiques,* vol. 2, p. 453.
5. Althusser, "On the Relations between Marx and Freud," *Writings on Psychoanalysis,* trans. J. Mehlman (New York: Columbia University Press, 1999).
6. In *Being and Nothingness* (1943), Sartre would declare the problem of solipsism (the problem of the reality of knowing anything outside the self) the fundamental problem of philosophy.
7. Carlo Bertolazzi, *El Nost Milan e altre commedie* (Turin: Einaudi, 1971).

For a detailed summary of the changes Strehler introduced, see Bernard Dort, "L'illusion de la vie quotidienne," *Théâtre public* (Paris: Éditions du Seuil, 1967), pp. 290–8.

8. Michael Sprinker, *Imaginary Relations* (New York: Verso, 1987).
9. Interestingly, Althusser singled out Alain Resnais's film *Muriel* for praise in his letters to Madonia. He reports having been "very moved" by this "admirable, truly admirable film." The film concerns the meeting of lovers separated by the war after a period of twenty years. They discover not only that they cannot recapture or even agree upon the facts of the past, their past, but that the present itself eludes them and us, the audience. ("They are not there. They were never there," writes Althusser) We are not sure who they are or what they do and Resnais' style of fragmentation and repetition serves both to confuse us and to make us weary of the inquiry. At the center of the film is a fundamental absence: the character Muriel. The stepson of the main female character has just returned from military service in Algeria. In the middle of the film, he begins to show home movies of his tour of duty: soldiers sitting in front of picturesque sights, palm trees, mosques, etc. or simply caught clowning around as if at a boys' camp. His voice-over narration is utterly at odds with the images on the screen, his screen, our screen. He tells us in uncomfortable detail of the arrest, torture and murder of a young resistance fighter in the Algerian war, whom he calls Muriel even though "that couldn't have been her name." She is the absent, deferred center of the film, unrepresented, unrepresentable, the truth off screen, the dialectic *à la cantonade* that forces us to leave the film in order to make sense of it, presenting us with an incompleteness that we take with us out of the cinema and into the world. She is also the synecdochic absent cause, the spirit invisible and inaudible that gathers itself and its forces throughout the film until, at the finale, it shatters our illusions and our myths about ourselves and our Western Civilization, which lie like shards of broken glass on desert sands.
10. See Pierre Macherey's first-hand account in *Histoire de dinosaure: faire de la philosophie, 1965–1997* (Paris: Presses Universitaires de France, 1999), p. 267.
11. See Michel Foucault, "Preface," *Dits et écrits*, vol. 1, 159–67.
12. The Fonds Althusser (the Althusser archive) at the Institute Mémoire de L'édition Contemporaine contains 600 pages of notes on Spinoza (Alt.2 A60–08), approximately 200 pages of which concern the *Tractatus Theologico-Politicus*.
13. Rashi is the acronym for Rabbi Solomon, son of Isaac (1040–1105). His extraordinary commentary on the Old Testament was the first attempt systematically to reconcile the contradictory passages and fill in the

gaps of Scripture. His commentary was included in the versions of the Old Testament studied in Jewish schools in the early modern period (each page would typically be divided between the Biblical passage and Rashi's commentary) and thus became indissociable from the text itself. In his discussion of Genesis 2:4, Rashi accords a meaning to the visual image of the letter ה which he says is open only on the bottom, showing either that all men descend towards death or that the wicked will surely fall.

14. David Hume, "Of the Standard of Taste," *Four Dissertations* (1757). Hume cites the story from *Don Quixote* of two men called upon to give their opinion of a cask of supposedly excellent wine. One pronounced it good, but for a certain strange taste of leather. The other passed a similar judgment, except for his insistence that the wine exhibited a certain taste of iron. Both were ridiculed by the general company until the cask was poured out and a key tied to a leather thong discovered. The work of art is that cask that can never be emptied; we must rely on the delicacy of the critic's taste for our judgments.
15. Beckett would write in *Molloy*: "You invent nothing, you think you are inventing, you think you are escaping, and all you do is stammer out your lesson, the remnants of a pensum one day got by heart and long forgotten, life without tears as it is wept" (Beckett 1976, 32).
16. Perhaps the purest example of such an approach is Roland Barthes's "Introduction to the Structural Analysis of Narratives" (1966) in *Image–Music–Text* (New York: Hill and Wang, 1977), pp. 79–124.
17. In chapter 9 of the *Tractatus Theologico-Politicus*, Spinoza points out that the Masoretes, the second-century Jewish scribes who in their zealousness to preserve the Scripture exactly as it was transmitted, not only counted the words and letters of each copy, but indicated where they believed a line or passage was missing. These empty spaces were themselves obscured in later versions of the Scripture, giving it the appearance of a coherence that it did not in fact possess. Spinoza cites the example of Genesis 4:8: "And Cain talked with Abel his brother: and it came to pass, when they were in the field, that Cain rose up against Abel his brother and slew him." The Masoretes argue that the motivation for or proximate cause of the murder (which later commentators would be at great pains to furnish) is lacking and that a phrase is missing. Spinoza holds that we will not know what Scripture really is until we recover these empty spaces and divest it of its false coherence and continuity.
18. It was posthumously published as Louis Althusser, *Sur la reproduction* (Paris: Presses Universitaires de France, 1995).

2 Some Concepts

The concept of history from Hegel to structuralism

Among Marx's great discoveries, for Althusser, was the necessary relation between the different areas of social life. From Hegel, Marx adopted the notion that politics, law, religion, art and economic life, far from existing in isolation from each other, each indifferent to the others, could not be understood except as part of a whole: the truth of any part could only be grasped at the level of the whole. In fact, in a rigorous sense, the various aspects of social life were only apparently separate aspects: each expressed in however disguised a form the essence of the whole. To know a historical period, then, was to reduce law, religion, and politics to the truth of which they were the appearance. Marx defended Hegel's concept of history against those who declared art or religion above politics or innocent of economic realities; Hegel at least compelled us to conceptualize the necessary relation between all the areas of social life.

Marx, however, modified Hegel's position in at least one crucial respect: the parts of the social whole could no longer be reduced to a truth that lay behind the material world; the necessary relation between the different aspects of society had to be understood as a relation between irreducibly different parts. No longer equivalent or identical, the different realms had to be understood in their specificity. For Marx, this meant that while all areas of social life were equally real, some were more determinant than others in making a given historical period what it was. In particular, the mode of economic production, the condition of any life at all, assigned to law, culture and politics their place in a given society.

Althusser sought to defend Marx's theoretical acquisitions against what he felt was a new version of Hegel's argument, structuralism. Like Hegel, certain structuralist thinkers saw each historical period as a self-contained system consisting of elements governed by rules, a fact that prevented them from explaining historical change. At the same time, Althusser argued that Marx's theory posed more problems than it answered: the nature of the causality by which society is determined to be what it is in its singularity remains to be specified. In particular he warned against any temptation to turn the economy into the truth to which every element in society could be reduced. To move things forward he proposed the notion of structural causality, a notion whose primary value lay in its excluding other theories of causality and pointing out the need for a new concept. Thus, the exploration of the precise relations between art, literature, politics and the sphere of production remains an imperative for any one who would develop Althusser's legacy.

Louis Althusser, Reading Capital

> The structure of the historical existence of the Hegelian social totality allows what I propose to call an "*essential section*" (*coupe d'essence*), i.e., an intellectual operation in which a *vertical break* is made at any moment in historical time, a break in the present such that all the elements of the whole revealed by this section are in an immediate relationship with one another, a relationship that immediately expresses their internal essence. When I speak of an "essential section", I shall therefore be referring to the specific structure of the social totality that allows this section, in which all the elements of the whole are given in a co-presence, itself the immediate presence of their essences, which thus become immediately *legible in them.* It is clear that it is the specific structure of the social totality which allows this essential section: for this section is only possible because of the peculiar nature of the unity of this totality, a "spiritual" unity, if we can express in this way the type of unity possessed by an expressive totality, i.e., a totality all of whose parts are so many *total parts,* each expressing the others, and each expressing the social totality that contains them, because each in itself contains in the immediate form of its expression the essence of the totality itself. I am referring to the structure of the Hegelian whole which I have already discussed: the Hegelian whole has a type of unity in which each element of the whole, whether material or economic determination, a political institution or a religious, artistic or philosophical form, is never anything more than the presence of the concept with itself at a historically determined moment. This is the sense in which the co-presence of the elements with one another and the presence of each element with the whole are based on a *de jure* preliminary

presence: the total presence of the concept in all the determinations of its existence. (95–6)

I have insisted on the nature of historical time and its theoretical conditions to this extent because this conception of history and of its relation to time is still alive amongst us, as can be seen from the currently widespread distinction between synchrony and diachrony. This distinction is based on a conception of historical time as continuous and homogeneous and contemporaneous with itself. The synchronic is contemporaneity itself, the co-presence of the essence with its determinations, the present being readable as a structure in an "essential section" because the present is the very existence of the essential structure. The synchronic therefore presupposes the ideological conception of a continuous–homogeneous time. It follows that the diachronic is merely the development of this present in the sequence of a temporal continuity in which the "events" to which "history" in the strict sense can be reduced (cf. Lévi-Strauss) are merely successive contingent presents in the time continuum. Like the synchronic, which is the primary concept, the diachronic therefore presupposes both of the very two characteristics I have isolated in the Hegelian conception of time: an ideological conception of historical time.

Ideological, because it is clear that this conception of historical time is merely a reflection of the conception Hegel had of the type of unity that constitutes the link between all the economic, political, religious, aesthetic, philosophical and other elements of the social whole. Because the Hegelian whole is a "spiritual whole" in the Leibnizian sense of a whole in which all the parts "conspire" together, in which each part is a *pars totalis*, the unity of this double aspect of historical time (homogeneous-continuity/contemporaneity) is possible and necessary. (96)

Humanism

The following key passage from *For Marx* is important in a number of respects. Althusser's critique of the idea of a human nature or essence goes far beyond Marx's argument that such theories deny not only the ways in which human beings are perpetually remade in history, their nature changing with the forms of production and exploitation, but that the projection of a fixed, unchanging character is no more than an unconscious reflection of the existing order, which, by declaring it eternal, sanctifies it. Marx even criticized those historians who argued that the history of previous epochs was no more than an anticipation of the present, which represented the fulfillment of what was before incomplete. For bourgeois historians, he commented, "there was history but there no longer is any."

Althusser's critique of humanism proceeds to demonstrate the paradoxes of the dominant form of humanism, individualism whether as an analytical or political concept. Individualism explains collective behavior by referring to the choices of the individuals who make it up. As Althusser points out, however, these individuals are all exactly alike in that they are expressions of an underlying essence (e.g., all individuals seek to maximize their utilities, to invoke one contemporary article of faith). Such a concept serves to obstruct any knowledge of individuals in the strict sense, that is, in their singularity, just as it prevents us from identifying the various forms of transindividuality that have emerged in history.

Louis Althusser, For Marx

> In 1845, Marx broke radically with every theory that based history and politics on an essence of man. This unique rupture contained three indissociable elements.
>
> The formation of a theory of history and politics based on radically new concepts: the concepts of social formation, productive forces, relations of production, superstructure, ideologies, determination in the last instance by the economy, specific determination of the other levels, etc.
>
> A radical critique of the *theoretical* pretensions of every philosophical humanism.
>
> The definition of humanism as an *ideology.*
>
> This new conception is completely rigorous as well, but it is a new rigour: the essence criticized (2) is defined as an ideology (3), a category belonging to the new theory of society and history (1).
>
> This rupture with every *philosophical* anthropology or humanism is no secondary detail; it is Marx's scientific discovery.
>
> It means that Marx rejected the problematic of the earlier philosophy and adopted a new problematic in one and the same act. The

earlier idealist ("bourgeois") philosophy depended in all its domains and arguments (its "theory of knowledge", its conception of history, its political economy, its ethics, its aesthetics, etc.) on a problematic of *human nature* (or the essence of man). For centuries, this problematic had been transparency itself, and no one had thought of questioning it even in its internal modifications.

This problematic was neither vague nor loose; on the contrary, it was constituted by a coherent system of precise concepts tightly articulated together. When Marx confronted it, it implied the two complementary postulates he defined in the Sixth Thesis on Feuerbach:

> That there is a universal essence of man;
>
> That this essence is the attribute of *each single individual* who is its real subject.

These two postulates are complementary and indissociable. But their existence and their unity presuppose a whole empiricist–idealist world outlook. If the essence of man is to be a universal attribute, it is essential that *concrete subjects* exist as absolute givens; this implies an *empiricism of the subject*. If these empirical individuals are to be men, it is essential that each carries in himself the whole human essence, if not in fact, at least in principle; this implies an *idealism of the essence*. So empiricism of the subject implies idealism of the essence and vice versa. This relation can be inverted into its "opposite" – empiricism of the concept/idealism of the subject. But the inversion respects the basic structure of the problematic, which remains fixed. (227–8)

Louis Althusser, Essays in Self-Criticism

One thing is certain: one cannot *begin* with man, because that would be to begin with a bourgeois idea of "man", and because the idea of *beginning with* man, in other words the idea of an absolute point of departure (= of an "essence") belongs to bourgeois philosophy. This idea of "man" as a starting-point, an absolute point of departure, is the basis of all bourgeois ideology; it is the soul of the great Classical Political Economy itself. "Man" is a myth of bourgeois ideology: Marxism–Leninism cannot *start* from "man". It starts "from the economically given social period"; and at the end of its analysis, when it "arrives", *it may find real men.* These men are thus the *point of arrival* of an analysis which starts from the social relations of the existing mode of production, from class relations, and from the class struggle. These men are quite different men from the "man" of bourgeois ideology.

> "Society is not *composed of individuals,*" says Marx. He is right: society is not a "combination", an "addition" of individuals. What constitutes society is the system of its social relations in which *its* individuals live, work and struggle. He is right: society is not made up of individuals in general, in the abstract, just so many copies of "man". Because each society has *its own* individuals, historically and socially determined. The slave-individual is not the serf-individual nor the each corresponding ruling class. In the same way, we must say that even a class is not "composed" of individuals in general: each class has *its own individuals,* fashioned in their individuality by their conditions of life, of work, of exploitation and of struggle – by the relations of the class struggle. In their mass, real men are what class conditions make of them. These conditions do not depend on bourgeois "human nature": liberty. On the contrary the liberties of men, including the forms and limits of these liberties, and including their will to struggle, depend on these conditions. (52–3)

Ideology

The juxtaposition of these two passages shows very clearly the shift in Althusser's conception of ideology between 1965 and 1970. Even the extract from *For Marx* shows the extent to which Althusser had transformed Marx's notion (even if he presents this transformation in the guise of a commentary on Marx). He begins by postulating that ideology is "a system of representations" in which knowledge is subordinated to political ends. In this early stage in Althusser's thought, science, consists of knowledge freed from any such subordination. Ideology as a system of representations which serves certain political ends is a definition fairly consonant with Marx's. From this relatively orthodox formula, however, Althusser draws some unexpected conclusions. Because ideology is a system, a system governed by rules, like, say, the system of language, we are compelled to recognize that no one exists outside these rules to impose them on others. In short the dominant class is every bit as bound by the rules as the dominated. As in the case of language, those who inhabit the system of representations obey the rules that govern it without knowing that what they believe to be their choice is in fact obedience to a rule; indeed, the rules they normally obey are unknown to them. Ideology is thus a matter not of consciousness but of the unconscious. This is as close as Althusser would come to structuralism; in fact, there are echoes here of the structural anthropology of Lévi-Strauss and others.

While in the 1965 text, Althusser had already begun to reconceptualize ideology in such a way that it was no longer primarily composed of ideas or even representations, but rather of actions and behaviors, the concept remained governed by a set of oppositions, imaginary/real, representation/realities, that left the material existence of ideology untheorized. It is in this sense that the ISAs (Ideological State Apparatuses) essay "Ideology and the state" is so important: Althusser changed everything but the name. Ideology is no longer a matter of minds, ideas or representations conscious or unconscious. Instead, ideology is the disposition of bodies in apparatuses, no longer a system but a war, a relation of opposing forces. The imaginary element of ideology, that by which we each believe ourselves to be the cause of what we do, is false, but nevertheless real and material. We are interpellated, addressed, judged and punished as the authors of our actions, our bodies caught in a very real apparatus of subjection.

Interestingly, in both texts Althusser maintains that there can be no society, no human history without ideology. He rejects the idea that such a notion is ahistorical; he prefers to call it transhistorical. In a tantalizing phrase, he first compares and then connects the transhistoricity of ideology to that of the unconscious (as understood by Lacan). Is the latter the condition of the former, as he seems sometimes to suggest? Or are both "co-terminous," perhaps explicable by a third term? Is it possible to understand the transhistoricity of ideology in other than Kantian terms as a distortion inherent in the very act of knowing? Again, there are elements of an answer scattered throughout the essay, as well as Althusser's other writings, but he nowhere gathers them together in a coherent whole.

Louis Althusser, "Marxism and Humanism," **For Marx**

> So everything depends on the knowledge of the nature of humanism as an ideology.
>
> There can be no question of attempting a profound definition of ideology here. It will suffice to know very schematically that an ideology is a system (with its own logic and rigour) of representations (images, myths, ideas or concepts, depending on the case) endowed with a historical existence and role within a given society. Without embarking on the problem of the relations between a science and its (ideological) past, we can say that ideology, as a system of representations, is distinguished from science in that in it the practico-social

function is more important than the theoretical function (function as knowledge). (231)

It is customary to suggest that ideology belongs to the region of "consciousness". We must not be misled by this appellation, which is still contaminated by the idealist problematic that preceded Marx. In truth, ideology has very little to do with "consciousness", even supposing this term to have an unambiguous meaning. It is profoundly *unsconcious*, even when it presents itself in a reflected form (as in pre-Marxist "philosophy"). Ideology is indeed a system of representations that have nothing to do with "consciousness": they are usually images and occasionally concepts, but it is above all as *structures* that they impose on the vast majority of men, not via their "consciousness". They are perceived–accepted–suffered cultural objects and they act functionally on men via a process that escapes them. Men "live" their ideologies as the Cartesian "saw" or did not see – if he was not looking at it – the moon two hundred paces away: *not at all as a form of consciousness, but as an object of their "world" – as their 'world' itself.* But what do we mean, then, when we say that ideology is a matter of men's "consciousness"? First, that ideology is distinct from other social instances, but also that men *live* their actions, usually referred to as freedom and "consciousness" by the classical tradition, in ideology, *by and through ideology*; in short, that the "lived" relation between men and the world, including History (in political action or inaction), passes through ideology, or better, *is ideology itself.* This is the sense in which Marx said that it is in ideology (as the locus of political struggle) that men *become conscious* of their place in the world and in history, it is within this ideological unconsciousness that men succeed in altering the "lived" relation between them and the world and acquiring that new form of specific unconsciousness called '"consciousness". (232–3)

Louis Althusser, "Ideology and the State," Lenin and Philosophy and Other Essays

Ideology has no history.

If eternal means, not transcendent to all (temporal) history, but omnipresent, trans-historical and therefore immutable in form throughout the extent of history, I shall adopt Freud's expression word for word, and write *ideology is eternal*, exactly like the unconscious. And I add that I find this comparison theoretically justified by the fact that the eternity of the unconscious is not unrelated to the eternity of ideology in general. (161)

Ideology is a "Representation" of the Imaginary Relationship of Individuals to their Real Conditions of Existence.

It is not their real conditions of existence, their real world, that "men" "represent to themselves" in ideology, but above all it is their relation to those conditions of existence which is represented to them there. It is this relation which is at the center of every ideological, i.e. imaginary, representation of the real world. Or rather, to leave aside the language of causality it is necessary to advance the thesis that it is the *imaginary nature of this relation* which underlies all the imaginary distortion that we can observe (if we do not live in its truth) in all ideology. (164)

Ideology has a material existence.

I shall therefore say that, where only a single subject (such and such individual) is concerned, the existence of the ideas of his belief is material in that *his ideas are his material actions inserted into material practices governed by material rituals which are themselves defined by the material ideological apparatus from which derive the ideas of that subject.* Naturally, the four inscriptions of the adjective modalities: the materialities of a displacement for going to mass, of kneeling down, of the gesture of the sign of the cross, or of the *mea culpa*, of a sentence, of a prayer, of an act of contrition, of a penitence, of a gaze, of a hand-shake, of an external verbal discourse or an "internal" verbal discourse (consciousness), are not one and the same materiality. I shall leave on one side the problem of a theory of the differences between the modalities of materiality. (169)

Ideology Interpellates Individuals as Subjects.

I say: the category of the subject is constitutive of all ideology, but at the same time and immediately I add that *the category of the subject is only constitutive of all ideology insofar as all ideology has the function (which defines it) of "constituting" concrete individuals as subjects.* In the interaction of this double constitution exists the functioning of all ideology, ideology being nothing but its functioning in the material forms of existence of that functioning. (171)

Creation/production

In this key passage, Macherey explores the implications of Althusser's critique of humanism for the study of literature. The idea of literary creation, in particular, captures the peculiar dependence of humanism, or philosophical anthropology, on the older model of theology. The author would possess all the attributes of a God, who depends on nothing, but on whom, in the realm of writing at least, all things depend. The author creates *ex nihilo*; there is nothing in his creation that does not originate in him. Even if we speak of influences, these are transformed in his private interiority into attributes of himself. In a very important sense, nothing comes before the gesture that fills the blank page with words. Conversely, if we would know the meaning of what is written we must turn to the subjectivity of the author in whom it originated. The notion of creation dehistoricizes and psychologizes the work of art.

In opposition, abandoning the figure of the Man–God, Macherey proposes the notion of literary production. The author writes only by virtue of taking up a place in a pre-existing process of production. The way the author writes as well as the materials used are determined by historical forces beyond the writer's will or control. The work is a product to be analyzed or deconstructed, no longer a mystery to be deciphered.

Pierre Macherey, **A Theory of Literary Production**

> The work is the product of a certain labour, and hence of an art. But not all art is artificial: it is the work of a labourer, and not of a conjurer or a showman. The power of this worker is not the false miracle of invoking an absolutely chosen form from nothing (this is why it is pointless to call the author a creator); and the scene of his labours is not a theatre – a stage for the presentation of some temporary decorative apparition. This is why he produces real determinate works. To speak of art as technique is to ignore its actual nature.
>
> The writer, as the producer of a text, does not manufacture the materials with which he works. Neither does he stumble across them as spontaneously available wandering fragments, useful in the building of any sort of edifice; they are not neutral transparent components which have the grace to vanish, to disappear into the totality they contribute to, giving it substance and adopting its forms. The causes that determine the existence of the work are not free implements, useful to elaborate any meaning: as we shall see in the course of a very definite example, they have a sort of specific weight, a peculiar power, which means that even when they are used and blended into a totality they retain a certain autonomy; and may, in some cases, resume their particular life. Not because there is some absolute and transcendent logic of aesthetic facts, but because their real

inscription in a history of forms means that they cannot be defined exclusively by their immediate function in a specific work. (41–2)

Now, art is not man's creation, it is a product (and the producer is not a subject centered in his creation, he is an element in a situation or a system): different – in being a product – from religion, which has chosen its dwelling among all the spontaneous illusions of spontaneity, which is certainly a kind of creation. Before disposing of these works – which can only be called theirs by an elaborate evasion – men have to *produce* them, not by magic, but by a real labour of production. If man creates man, the artist produces works, *in determinate conditions*; he does not work on himself but on that thing which escapes him in so many ways, and never belongs to him until after the event.

The various "theories" of creation all ignore the process of making; they omit any account of production. One can create undiminished, so, paradoxically, creation is the release of what is already there; or, one is witness of a sudden apparition, and then creation is an interruption, an epiphany, a mystery. In both instances any possible explanation of the change has been done away with: in the former, nothing has happened; and in the latter what has happened is inexplicable. All speculation over man the creator is intended to eliminate a real knowledge: the "creative process" is, precisely, not a process, a labour; it is a religious formula to be found on funeral monuments.

For the same reasons, all considerations of genius, of the subjectivity of the artist, of his soul, are *on principle* uninteresting.

You will understand why, in this book, the word "creation" is suppressed, and systematically replaced by "production". (67–8)

Symptomatic reading

When we reject the idea, the model, of the work as an expression of an intention (whether individual or collective, a matter of content or form) which would then serve as the meaning to be discovered in it, the essence which everything about the work would disclose, if read correctly, our very sense of the text is transformed. In the absence of a transcendental term to which a reading would reduce the only apparent diversity of the text, the work becomes a mere surface deprived of any depth, its contradictions and discrepancies placed clearly and inescapably in relief. We can no longer resolve or explain away the disorder of the text; we can only explain why it is what it is in its very disorder. Thus, the traditional vocabulary of literary criticism is insufficient. A vocabulary adequate to the task of explaining the unresolved, unfinished and scattered nature of the work is required. Both Althusser and Macherey begin by borrowing concepts from psychoanalysis: repression, displacement, splitting. Every literary or philosophical text says more than it wants to say or knows that it says. At the same time, these symptoms are not expressions of some primal disorder, a transcendental principle of the negative. The contradictions that works exhibit are historically determined; to identify and explain them is to understand the history of which they are a part.

Louis Althusser, Reading Capital

> The same connexion that defines the visible also defines the invisible as its shadowy obverse. It is the field of the problematic that defines and structures the invisible as the defined excluded, *excluded* from the field of visibility and *defined* as excluded by the existence and peculiar structure of the field of the problematic; as what forbids and represses the reflection of the field on its object, i.e., the necessary and immanent inter-relationship of the problematic and one of its objects. This is the case with oxygen in the phlogistic theory of chemistry, or with surplus value and the definition of the "value of labour" in classical economics. These new objects and problems are necessarily *invisible* in the field of the existing theory, because they are not objects of this theory, because they are forbidden by it – they are objects and problems necessarily without any necessary relations with the field of the visible as defined by this problematic. They are invisible because they are rejected in principle, repressed from the field of the visible: and that is why their fleeting presence in the field when it does occur (in very peculiar and symptomatic circumstances) *goes unperceived,* and becomes literally an undivulgeable absence since the whole function of the field is not to see them, to forbid any sighting of them. Here again, the invisible is no more a function of *a subject's sighting* than is the visible: the invisible is the darkness, the blinded eye of the theoretical problematic's self-reflection when it scans its non-objects, its non-problems, without seeing them, *in order not to look at them.* (25–6)

Pierre Macherey, A Theory of Literary Production

> We should question the work as to what it does not and cannot say, in those silences for which it has been made. The concealed order of

> the work is thus less significant than its real determinate disorder (its disarray). The order which it professes is merely an imagined order, projected on to disorder, the fictive resolution of ideological conflicts, a resolution so precarious that it is obvious in the very letter of the text where incoherence and incompleteness burst forth. (155)

Philosophy as intervention

The passage below captures in a particularly colorful and evocative way Althusser's conception of what it is to do or to practice philosophy or theory. Why does Althusser employ this somewhat unfamiliar terminology to describe what is often thought of as a metadiscourse whose role is, from outside the field it considers, to test the coherence of arguments and adjudicate competing claims? According to this conception, philosophy would function as a superior or supreme court of reason, the final arbiter of truth. In opposition, Althusser argued that philosophy in no way transcends the field it is considering and does not operate in a vacuum, unaffected by the history around it. Instead philosophy is a particular kind of practice among other practices and exists in a very precisely determined historical moment. Because, for Althusser, every historical moment is a conjuncture of divergent and opposing forces, philosophy whether it wants to or not, whether it openly declares its partisanship or claims neutrality, takes a position in the configuration of forces that characterize a specific historical situation. All philosophy is entangled in social struggles.

While many philosophies deny their historical belonging, all in fact constitute interventions. A philosophical doctrine emerges in an already occupied space and must displace the doctrines that precede it. The field of philosophy, then, becomes a battlefield although the battle is not fought between two clearly demarcated camps, bourgeois and proletarian, dominant and dominated. Rather, the field of philosophy is divided into a multiplicity of forces arranged into always temporary alliances, struggling against each other in ways that are not clearly understood until after the fact. It was in this way that Althusser came to see philosophy as an adventure full of risks or surprises, in which victory could never be guaranteed in advance.

Louis Althusser, Essays in Self-Criticism

A philosophy does not make its appearance in the world as Minerva appeared to the society of Gods and men. It only exists in so far as it occupies a position, and it only occupies this position in so far as it has conquered it in the thick of an already occupied world. It therefore only exists in so far as this conflict has made it something distinct, and this distinctive character can only be won and imposed in an indirect way, by a detour involving ceaseless study of other, existing positions. This detour is the form of the conflict which determines what side a philosophy takes in the battle and on the "kampfplatz" (Kant), the battlefield which is philosophy. Because if the philosophy of philosophers is this perpetual war (to which Kant wanted to put an end by introducing the everlasting peace of his own philosophy), then no philosophy can exist within this theoretical relation of force except in so far as it marks itself off from its opponents and lays siege to that part of the positions which they have had to occupy in order to guarantee their power over the enemy whose impress they bear. If – as Hobbes says, speaking perhaps to empty benches, and with reference as much to philosophy as to the society of men – war is a generalized state, and leaves nowhere in the world for a shelter, and if it produces its own condition as its own result, which means that every war is essentially *preventative*, it is possible to understand that the war of philosophies, in which systems come into conflict, presupposes the preventative strike of positions against one another, and thus the necessary use by a philosophy of a detour *via* other philosophies in order to define and defend its own positions. (165–6)

3 Readings

Wild crowds, savage movements: *Heart of Darkness* and the rise of International Socialism

In his remarkable study of colonial rule in the Congo from the mid-1880s until the beginning of the First World War, *King Leopold's Ghost,* Adam Hochschild issues the following challenge to scholars who would take *Heart of Darkness* as an object of study:

> High school teachers and college professors who have discussed this book in thousands of class rooms over the years tend to do so in terms of Freud, Jung and Nietzsche; of classical myth, Victorian innocence and original sin; of postmodernism, postcolonialism, and post-structuralism. European and American readers, not comfortable acknowledging the genocidal scale of the killing in Africa at the turn of the century, have cast *Heart of Darkness* loose from its historical moorings. We read it as a parable for all times and all places, not as a book about one time and place. (143)

To take Hochschild's challenge seriously, as I believe we should, that is, to refuse to separate Conrad's work from the history that made it possible, however, immediately confronts us with the fact that he has posed a problem or a question without giving us either an answer or the means by which we might arrive at an answer.

Let us take the elements of an answer he proposes: we should read *Heart of Darkness* as a novel "about one time and one place" of which it is, moreover, a "precise and detailed . . . description" (ibid., 143). Should we assume that what Conrad's novel "is about" is the same thing as "its historical moorings"? To put it another way, the work is *of* a specific time and place, the historical situation in which it was produced. Must what it is about, what it describes, be that same situation? We need only recall that *Heart of Darkness* was not written during Conrad's sojourn in the Congo in 1890, but fully eight years later in London. Further, the text of the journal Conrad kept in Africa is notable precisely for a paucity of description, especially of African scenery, people, culture, or language. Even more interestingly, while Hochschild cites the passage in *Heart of Darkness* in which Conrad does indeed describe slave labor in detail, as many readers have noted, he also repeatedly uses language that he himself described as "foggy," thus depriving the people as well as the landscape of any specificity. This observation allows us, in turn, to hypothesize that the ahistorical readings of the novel so common, as Hochschild rightly remarks, are not accidental, a collective misreading of which the novel would be entirely innocent. To take the hypothesis even further, we can say that the very way in which the novel casts shadows over what it purports to describe determines its political effects. Most of the scenes Hochschild cites as reasonably accurate representations of colonial barbarism occur towards the beginning of Marlow's stay in the Congo; at that point the reader indeed feels sympathy for the African and revulsion at the colonizers. Whether the reader will continue to do so is another question. Indeed, Conrad appears to cast a pall of darkness over everything, burying colonizer and colonized, torturer and victim, good and bad alike in an impenetrably black night.

Even more important is the question of how we go about reading *Heart of Darkness* historically: do we reconstruct the history of the Congo *c.* 1890, to the point of seeking the "originals" of the novel's places and characters? Such an approach begins with history and confronts the novel only to reduce it to its referents. Moreover, is it enough to situate the work in the history of the Congo? After all, this history itself (not to mention the narrative, which begins and ends on a boat on the Thames in London) is unintelligible except insofar as it is connected to other histories: the history of European imperialism in Africa (but why only in Africa?), the causes of imperialism itself, the history of resistance to imperialism in Africa and Europe, etc. The list could be expanded indefinitely: are we then to abandon the task of reading the text historically as impractical?

The answer of course is No, but such a reading can only be undertaken if we accept as our starting point the irreducible materiality of the text. To regard the text as a historical artifact is to refuse to take it as a mere reflection of a reality completely external to it to which it might be returned (as if finding the "real" Kurtz would settle any of the many controversies raised by the novel). On the contrary, we must enter into the text itself, its words, its sentences, and read it to the letter. After all, history is in the work as well as outside of it; it is only by unraveling the threads of which it is woven that we can then follow them outward to other texts and other histories. We cannot read *Heart of Darkness* all at once, however; nor in a relatively brief essay can we proceed from the beginning to the end of the narrative. Instead, let us take a sample, a specific passage whose properties will allow us to begin to outline the complexities of its historical determination. It might be feared that such a procedure will once again, as Hochschild worried, lead us away from the uncomfortable facts of European imperialist domination of Africa, that legacy of genocide, slavery and famine that his book, along with other recent studies, so admirably documents. In fact, such an approach will contribute to our understanding of the ideologies inextricably bound up with the actual practices of those nations that accounted themselves civilized in Africa.

Near the end of his narrative, Marlow visits Kurtz's Intended. The sun is setting as he is ushered into her apartment and Marlow notes repeatedly, at least every few paragraphs, that as she speaks the darkness deepens; by the conclusion of their meeting night has fallen. At this point, the end of *Heart of Darkness*, the reader once again confronts the fact that Marlow's narrative has been repeated to us, that it is one long citation by the unnamed narrator. The final scene of Marlow's narrative is thus doubly complicated as the narrator cites Marlow citing her speech. Unlike the anonymous narrator, however, Marlow frequently interposes himself between his audience and the Intended's speech: he reproduces only fragments of what she says, each separated and accompanied by his commentary, telling his audience the thoughts and memories that remained untold to her, that her words stirred up in him. He makes no effort to connect the fragments he reproduces: she is halted in the middle of one sentence, only to resume in the middle of another, the breaks marked by a dash and often resumed after an ellipsis. In the case we will examine, the disruption of the Intended's narrative works to ironic effect, making visible the contradictions in her account of Kurtz of which she herself is unaware.

"She talked as thirsty men drink" because, since the death of Kurtz's mother, she has had "no one – to – to – " (Conrad 1983, 108). The sentence breaks off at this point and we are left to infer that she has had no one to talk to about Kurtz, no one with whom she may share her memories and feelings. Her own people, we learn in the next paragraph, disapproved of her engagement to Kurtz, given his "comparative poverty." In the context of her isolation, the absence of a world of friends and loved ones to mourn Kurtz with her, the particular way her narrative resumes (its resumption is marked by an ellipsis) appears all the more paradoxical and problematic: " . . . 'Who was not his friend who had heard him speak once?' She was saying. 'He drew men towards him by what was best in them.'" Although she continues to speak, her voice is drowned out or written over by Marlow's. There thus appears at this point an ironic disjunction: the man who drew others to him, dies nearly friendless, mourned by only two people.

The fact remains, however, that Kurtz indeed possessed a strange power of speech, a very real capacity to assemble multitudes around him in a way that had little to do with friendship. His voice could indeed cause crowds to materialize out of thin air; he could gather together a thousand dispersed individuals into one ominous mass and it was this, above all, that made him the agent of a threatening darkness. The men united by and through his words were not drawn from the polite society of Europe; they were those in fact whose very gathering together in a group constitutes them as the object of fear; they are the mob, the wild crowd whose numbers alone pose a threat to order and rationality. By invoking Kurtz's ability not only to assemble but to influence a crowd, the Intended invokes without knowing it the powers of darkness that flow through the savage wilderness and its savage men, through Kurtz:

> the sound of her low voice seemed to have the accompaniment of all the other sounds, full of mystery, desolation, and sorrow, I had ever heard – the ripple of the river, the soughing of the trees swayed by the wind, the murmurs of the crowds, the faint ring of incomprehensible words cried from afar, the whisper of a voice speaking from beyond the threshold of an eternal darkness. (Ibid., 108)

Before examining this passage in detail, however, it is helpful to note the single change Conrad made in the text. In the manuscript, the *Blackwood's Magazine* version of 1899 and the Blackwood's book version of 1902, "crowds" is modified by the adjective "wild", which Conrad suppressed in the 1917 edition; all subsequent editions have preserved this deletion. Is it possible to assign any significance to this apparently slight change to the text? The passage is an important one: it anticipates and prepares the reader for the conclusion of Marlow's narrative and summarizes in a particularly euphonious way all that has gone before. The Intended's words, which contain the meaning she has imparted to them, are accompanied by mere sounds, inhuman, meaningless or whose meaning is the absence of meaning. Her language is haunted by sounds and noises which, although seemingly conjured up by her speech, confer by their presence a meaning upon it that is in utter contrast to what she thinks she means. The force of Marlow's narrative, now nearing its conclusion, compels us to go even further: the very distinction between "her low voice" and "all the other sounds" that accompany it is itself a fiction, the fiction that the human is distinct from the natural or, for that matter, civilization from savagery. It is, however, a necessary fiction, as necessary as the lie that Marlow tells her to keep the darkness and horror at bay. The description of that which accompanies her words, however, merits an even closer examination. It is easy to lose sight of the fact that the passage cited above consists of a single sentence, a fact that gives it the appearance perhaps of a continuity of meaning that it, upon scrutiny, does not possess. Further, this appearance of homogeneity of meaning is enacted at the level of sound: the passage exhibits perhaps the highest incidence of alliteration and assonance in a novel whose frequent recourse to these devices irritated more than a few readers over the years.

The sentence changes rather markedly after the dash that separates the description of the Intended's voice from the description of what seems to accompany her. The alliteration only faintly present prior to it (the repetition of "s" sounds) becomes much more pronounced: the repetition of "r" in "the ripple of the river" and again "s" in "the soughing of trees swayed." Just as we begin insensibly to expect alliteration, however, it is disrupted by the abrupt hard "c" in "the murmurs of the crowds" (linked later by sound to the adjective "incomprehensible" and the verb "cried"), an abruptness that the addition of "wild," to "crowds," echoing "wind" before it and "words" and "whisper" after it, had the effect of softening. Read in isolation, the phrases "ripple of the river" and "soughing of the the trees swayed by the wind" do not communicate either desolation or sorrow; on the contrary, there is a musicality to the phrases that almost appears designed to imitate a natural music. One could imagine (and probably find) them in a pastoral poem of a century earlier ("soughing" is already a bit archaic and "countrified"). They take on the sinister meaning Conrad seeks to imbue them with only as elements in a series that progresses from innocence to evil. Ripple, soughing, murmurs: the reader almost expects the third noun in the series to denote another natural entity and instead finds the discordant "crowds." Its place in the sentence links the crowd to other natural entities and elemental forces: blowing winds and rushing rivers. Moreover, "ripple," "soughing" and "murmurs" are onomatopoeic words, that not only denote a sound but imitate or reproduce it; they are among the exceptional cases in which an actual sound in nature determines the sound of a word.

The effect of all of this is to naturalize "crowds," which in this passage are deprived of their properly human character and transformed into the equivalent of the river and trees, a naturalization that Conrad extends to other terms denoting the forms of human collectivity. Thus, the word "mob" appears only twice in *Heart of Darkness.* Once, significantly, as a synonym for the crowd stirred to collective utterance at Kurtz's departure, by his African mistress: "She put out her hands, shouted something, and all that wild mob took up the shout in a roaring chorus of articulated, rapid, breathless utterance (ibid., 96). "Mob" appears only one other time: the river flows through a "mob of wooded islands," a place where "vegetation rioted." "Crowd" in the singular or plural occurs only eight times in *Heart of Darkness.* In one scene the crowd, no longer even animate, but more like inorganic matter moved by forces external to it, is described as "streams of human beings . . . poured into the clearing by the dark-faced and pensive forest" (ibid., 85). When the crowd vanishes, it does so "without any perceptible movement of retreat, as if the forest that had ejected these beings so suddenly had drawn them in again as the breath is drawn in a long aspiration" (ibid., 86). Even when the crowd undertakes a decisive action in attacking the steamer that has come to take Kurtz, its action, far from giving it a human aspect by reminding us that it is composed of individuals, transforms it into a mass of separated fragments, not even bodies, but parts of bodies, each moving itself: "suddenly, as though a veil had been removed from from my eyes, I made out, deep in the tangled gloom, naked breasts, arms, legs, glaring eyes, – the bush was swarming with human limbs in movement. . . . I saw vague forms of men running bent double, leaping, gliding, indistinct, incomplete, evanescent" (ibid., 64–5). The nouns and verbs conventionally linked to the forms of collective action are used to suggest the chaos and disorder of nature, of which by a kind of relay effect these very forms of collective action become the expressions; from now on "crowds," "mobs" and "masses" serve to suggest the violent eruption of the inhuman within humanity itself, as if paradoxically the crowd is the privileged site of the division and dissociation of humanity from itself.

In this way, the utterance produced by crowds both is and is not speech; if their murmurs can be divided into parts of speech, including words, it is speech that is doomed to remain incomprehensible, speech that cannot communicate in the sense of bearing meaning, but only "cries from afar," from a distance so great that no meaning can traverse it. The linking by sound of "crowd," "incomprehensible" and "cried" in the passage with which we began makes the crowd as unintelligible as the face of brute nature, swept by passions as powerful and uncontrollable as raging storms. Finally, the series (and the sentence) ends with that voice that conjures up the crowd, commands it to be still or to move, to attack or to retreat and which can make the crowd vanish as suddenly as it appeared. But "the whisper of a voice from beyond the threshold of an eternal darkness" is a disembodied voice which does not, if we follow the pattern of resemblances in the novel, belong exclusively to Kurtz. The African woman too can agitate the crowd, sending it into a frenzy or dispersing it into the bush.

In fact, the sentence repeats almost verbatim entire phrases from an earlier passage: the moment alluded to in the description of the Intended's "accompaniment" when Kurtz boards the steamer to return to the Company station:

> When next day we left at noon, the crowd, of whose presence behind a curtain of trees I had been acutely conscious all the time, flowed out of the woods again, filled the clearing, covered the slope with a mass of naked, breathing, quivering, bronze bodies. . . . They shouted periodically together strings of amazing words that resembled no sounds of human language; and the deep murmurs of the crowd, interrupted suddenly, were like the responses of some satanic litany. (Ibid., 96)

The Intended's expression of loss thus recalls that of "the wild mob" that attends Kurtz's departure from the interior, a voice incomprehensible, divested of meaning. "Murmurs of the crowds": Marlow's recollection of the earlier scene repeats the phrase with one small difference: the singular crowd becomes plural at the conclusion of the narrative, the crowd becomes crowds. It is at this point that the suppression of "wild," changing "wild crowds" simply to "crowds," can perhaps be accorded a certain significance. The plural of crowds suggests that Marlow hears not simply the accompaniment of that crowd from that fatal day up river, but the murmurs of other crowds as well. After 1917, the narrative no longer compels us to limit our associations to "wild," savage, African crowds. But what other crowds are present in the novel?

Let us recall that Marlow's remembrances begin with the Intended's evocation of Kurtz's powers of speech, his ability to draw men to him and around him. Marlow too experienced this power: the wild crowds immobilized by his words or swirling around Kurtz in a kind of frenzy of adoration. But this very association of crowds with Kurtz's oratorical prowess connects to an often overlooked scene just prior to Marlow's meeting with the Intended. After Marlow's return to the "sepulchral city," among the visitors who come to inquire about Kurtz, "a journalist anxious to know something of the fate of his 'dear colleague' turned up" (ibid., 104). The visitor confesses to Marlow that Kurtz, nominally a journalist, "really couldn't write a bit – 'but heavens! how that man could talk' " (ibid., 104). He argues that "Kurtz's proper sphere ought to have been politics 'on the popular side'. . . . He would have made a splendid leader of an extreme party" (ibid., 104). Moreover, the visitor tells Marlow that Kurtz "electrified large meetings." Writing appears here as the rational form of communication and its rationality resides at least in part in the fact that it is typically read individually, in isolation. Kurtz "really couldn't write a bit"; his province is instead oratory, speaking to crowds at mass meetings. His speech "electrifies," an industrial metaphor reserved for European crowds that nevertheless conveys a sense of the power that Kurtz's addresses send surging through the mass. A "meeting" of course is not a wild mob, unless, that is, it is moved to violent acts by inflammatory words.

An extreme party on the popular side, large meetings: to what does Conrad refer here, in a passage as oblique as any, in a novel that has been described even by those with the highest regard for Conrad as "murky" and "foggy"? The novel gives the reader no clues. An absence, an empty space thus becomes visible, the absent equivalent of Kurtz's African crowd and its unspeakable rites. This equivalent is not hidden: we would seek for it in vain in the pages of *Heart of Darkness*, where it is present only in the form of a lack. It is this lack, however, that marks the insufficiency and incompleteness of the text: to remain in it we must go outside of it to other texts from which it cannot totally be separated, and to the history that it displays without knowing it (the history of imperialism certainly, but the histories that are interwoven with that history as well). Perhaps it is the absent presence of this history that gives the novel what E. M. Forster called "a central obscurity," arguing that Conrad's work in general is "misty in the middle as well as at the edges" (indeed, Conrad himself referred to the "fogginess of H. of D."). F. R. Leavis lamented, but we may take as symptomatic, the frequency of such adjectives as "inconceivable," "inexpressible," and "unspeakable." The darkness of the novel itself comes to resemble what Hegel called that dark night in which all cows are black, a darkness in which distinctions and differences become invisible. This darkness, however, may be nothing more than the novel's "inner darkness of exclusion."

The voice that speaks from beyond the threshold of eternal darkness, the voice that makes crowds materialize out of nowhere and impels them into speech and action, is audible in a number of Conrad's works from the same period. One in particular, written at most a year or two before *Heart of Darkness*, seems particularly significant in this regard: *The Nigger of the Narcissus*. There blackness is not the engulfing surrounding menace of *Heart of Darkness*; on the contrary, it is localized in a single character, James Wait, a black sailor from the West Indies. The fact that the blackness exists only in a single man, alone among a white, European crew, makes it no less destructive, however. Wait, a malingerer and a shirker who feigns illness while collecting his wages, becomes through his ability to excite the sympathy of his fellows the principle of corruption on the ship. But corruption of what? For many critics, Conrad privileges the world of the ship as a kind of ideal community, a world of solidarity where in the face of the power of the sea, individual sailors depend on each performing the duties allotted to him on the ship. *The Nigger of the Narcissus*, however, suggests, despite itself, exactly the contrary: the world of the ship is or should be a largely silent world of work: the loyalty of the ship's company, the narrator tells us, is "unspoken," its faith "unexpressed" (Conrad 1975, 21). The space the crew occupies is a segmented, cellular space: in the forecastle every man retires to his bunk; the best among them do not speak but engage in silent meditation. Those who speak are suspect; their speech threatens the order of the ship. Jimmy's sick bay cabin becomes an alternate space in which the crew mingle and talk. As a consequence, Conrad's narrator complains,

> Through him we were becoming highly humanized, tender, complex, excessively decadent: we understood the subtlety of his fear, sympathized with all his repulsions, shrinkings, evasions, delusions – as though we were becoming over-civilized and rotten, and without any knowledge of the meaning of life. (Ibid., 117)

Sympathy (which might be thought to be the precondition of any genuine solidarity) is dangerous; the capacity to feel the sufferings of another, to be bound together in a community of feeling, leads by an inescapable logic to resistance and revolt against authority.

The voice that unites a collectivity on the *Narcissus*, however, is not the electrifying voice of a mass orator; it speaks through Jimmy's soulmate, Donkin, a fellow shirker who isn't man enough in the eyes of Conrad's narrator to withstand the corporal discipline of the ship's officers, the over-work and half-rations, and who whines, squeaks, and snivels. "He knew," however, "how to conquer the naive instincts of that crowd" (ibid., 22). When the Captain refuses to allow Jimmy to work, even when the latter is willing to do so, and orders him below for the remainder of the voyage, the men rise in revolt. Donkin, the agitator, steps in:

> "Are we bloomin' masheens?" inquired Donkin in a piercing tone, and dived under the elbows of the front rank. "Show 'im we ain't boys . . ." – "The man's a man if he is black" – "We ain't goin' to work this bloomin' ship shorthanded if Snowball's all right . . . " – "He says he is" – "Well, then, strike, boys, strike!" [ellipses in the original]

The crew in revolt is described in terms nearly identical to those Conrad employs to describe the African crowd:

> "a dark mass stamped, eddied, advanced, retreated. . . . Gesticulating arms, profiles of heads with open mouths appeared for a moment in the illuminated squares of doorways; black fists darted – withdrew . . . "Yes. It was most damnable to have such an unprovoked row sprung on one," assented the master. (Ibid., 107)

The mutiny fails and Donkin who, according to the narrator, "never did a decent day's work in his life" is given a dishonorable discharge upon their return to England. He is forced to give up the sea and "no doubt earns his living by discoursing with filthy eloquence upon the right of labor to live" (ibid., 143).

"The Secret Sharer," another text from the same period (written a few years after *Heart of Darkness*), is similarly constructed around the problem of authority in the face of mutinous crews. Leggatt, the secret sharer of a first-time captain of a freighter, has been forced to flee his own ship after killing one of the crew, a killing that the narrative constructs as justified. The victim is described in terms very similar to those Conrad applies to Donkin in *The Nigger of the Narcissus*:

> He was one of those creatures that are just simmering all the time with a silly sort of wickedness. Miserable devils that have no business to live at all. He wouldn't do his duty and wouldn't let anybody else do theirs. But what's the use of talking! You know well enough the sort of ill-conditioned snarling cur – (Conrad 1962, 319)

Leggatt goes on to say that after suffering some of the man's "cursed insolence . . . I turned round and felled him like an ox. He up and at me . . . I had him by the throat, and went on shaking him like a rat . . . I was holding him by the throat still when the picked us up. He was black in the face" (ibid., 320). The captain and narrator understands immediately that although illegal, Leggatt's act was morally justified.

If Conrad's ships are microcosmic societies, then they show the way that every society, insofar as it assembles men together to labor, remains inescapably haunted by the specter of revolt, mutiny and the strike. Further, when sailors revolt they are marked by the narrative as inhuman: they are animals and they are, significantly, black. In this sense, the crew of thirty cannibals Marlow enlists to man the steamer is emblematic: every crew embodies a latent savagery that waits only for the right weather or conditions to make itself manifest. The cannibals, from whom Marlow would "just as soon have expected restraint" as from a "hyena prowling amongst the corpses of a battlefield," given that they outnumber the Europeans on board by thirty to five and could easily overwhelm them, turn their hunger towards the fellows on the shore rather than their "superiors." Marlow cannot explain their forbearance, which is nothing other than the seemingly inexplicable forbearance of all those who suffer, in the absence of any coercion, deprivation and exploitation, to benefit others. For Conrad this is the mystery of obedience and loyalty to one's superiors, a mystery that, as he reminds us in *The Nigger of the Narcissus,* remains inexpressible. And as is the case with every mysticism, there lurks the fear that the ineffable is no more than an abyss over which everything so precariously hovers and into which it may be hurled by the slightest of disturbances.

It is instructive in this regard to contrast Conrad's treatment of Africans in *Heart of Darkness* to that in his only other fictional treatment of the Congo, "An Outpost of Progress" (1897), often regarded as an early draft of *Heart of Darkness.* There, certain Africans have proper names and function as characters with speaking roles. Moreover, there is no cannibalism in the Congo of "An Outpost of Progress" (apparently the human sacrifice there attributed to some tribes was insufficient to produce the effect Conrad sought), and Africans are depicted (accurately, I should add) as a primarily agricultural people who supply the outpost with yams, fowl and palm wine. They possess firearms, which although antiquated, require ammunition and powder or at least the materials to manufacture them. The Africans, then, in "An Outpost of Progress," no matter how inferior to the whites, are in no way prehistoric; on the contrary they are fully integrated into the world market or at least that part of it centered in the trading complex of the Indian Ocean. They thus differ to a striking degree from the cannibalistic hunter-gatherers of *Heart of Darkness,* which, by depriving them of names and personalities, renders the Africans an indistinguishable mass barely capable of human speech and perhaps closer to the animal than to the human.

This is not the impressionism that some readers have attributed to Conrad, as if the portrait of the Africans in *Heart of Darkness* were a kind of Monet *en noir.* It is not simply that Conrad chooses to render them less distinct, creating a kind of prose *chiaoscuro.* He very precisely bestializes them, picturing in great detail their filed teeth and splay feet, but omitting any attempt to reproduce their language, preferring instead regularly to remind us of their grunts. This rhetorical strategy produces certain effects: the reader feels sympathy for them only up to the precise point in the novel when Marlow turns away from the dying slave laborers to resume his duties, a gesture of resignation and acceptance that continues to the end of his narrative, where he will lie to protect the only civilization we have. It is difficult, to say the least, as Chinua Achebe ventured to remind Conrad scholars a quarter of a century ago, to extend one's sympathy to "a dog in a parody of breeches and a feather hat, walking on his hind legs." In fact, the progress of the narrative forces the reader, with Marlow, to revise his hasty judgment, upon arriving at the station, that the slave laborers chained together couldn't be called enemies or criminals. How else are we to regard what he will soon inform us are the cannibal savages?

Further, the contrasting depiction of Africans noted above allows us to move beyond a denunciation of Conrad for failing faithfully to reproduce historical reality, to an explanation of its ideological function. Through the mediation of the character of Kurtz, a kind of parallelism, a set of equivalences, however, begins to emerge: wild crowds, large meetings; spellbound and electrified audiences, savages and popular politics. To make visible this set of equivalences, however, we must place *Heart of Darkness* in the context of Conrad's other works, especially those in which, as we have noted, blackness and revolt commingle: the blackness at the heart of the mutiny on board the *Narcissus* and the blackening of the men in revolt; the blackened face of the insolent rebel in the hands of Leggatt. *Heart of Darkness* not only adds to their number, it gives this motif a whole new dimension, linking the savagery at the core to the savagery at the periphery, ultimately repudiating the notion that savagery, while at the historical origin of civilized society (an origin made visible by those distant prehistoric places) and caged still deep within, is contained by the surface truths, i.e., lies, that allow us to live. Nor is it the case that *Heart of Darkness* presents us with an allegory of the savagery internal to Europe in the guise of African savagery. It is rather that the wild crowds and savage movements, African and European alike, are equally real and, even more importantly, linked together in Conrad's narratives by a set of resemblances and in history by the emergence of socialist and anti-colonial mass movements at the precise moment when imperialism provoked large-scale resistance in the African colonies (Boahen). In the same way, the millions slain by British, German and French armies in Africa in the nearly twenty-five-year period between Conrad's voyage to the Congo (1890) and the outbreak of the First World War would have their civilized counterparts soon enough, as military commanders gained valuable experience in the techniques of mass extermination (Vandervort 1998, 185–208).

The precise nature of the European savagery, however, remains to be specified. Let us return to Kurtz, whose voice draws men around him, who sets wild crowds and savage movements into action, the man whose proper destiny would have been as leader of an extremist party on the popular side: *Heart of Darkness* is inscribed in the period 1889–1917, the period of the spectacular rise of mass movements of labor, of the working class. As Conrad was preparing for his voyage to the Congo, the London docks became the site of one of the most important strikes in British history, the Dockers' strike of 1889. Naturally, the effects of the strike were felt throughout the maritime industry and the Sailors' and Firemen's union experienced explosive growth, bringing about important changes in shipboard life (these struggles are certainly woven into *The Nigger of the Narcissus* where, as we have seen, Conrad is at great pains to sneer at "the rights of labor"). These, together with other developments in the working class (strikes as well as organized protest against unemployment), led to the emergence of the Independent Labour Party, the first mass electoral party of the working class. Internationally, Conrad's journey to the Congo coincided with the constitution of the Second International (1889), the coordinating body for socialist parties that had arisen elsewhere at the same time.

The Socialist International at its founding called for the abolition of capitalism worldwide and for the collective, democratically controlled ownership of industry. The International instructed its member parties to prepare for a general strike and instituted May Day as the Day of the Worker. May Day, 1890, in London, saw a demonstration of nearly 200,000 workers and was hailed by an elderly Friedrich Engels as the moment of the awakening of the British working class.

Moreover, the Second International in general and British socialists in particular had quite strong views on colonialism. As Hochschild shows in detail, it was common for humanitarians and religious leaders to express publicly their outrage at the abuses committed in the colonies of other nations. Thus the German press might run cartoons depicting King Leopold of Belgium surrounded by skulls; their outrage, however, did not extend to their own army in Germany's African colonies, which in 1904 slaughtered in a few weeks 80 percent of the Herero people in Southwest Africa (now Namibia) or 60,000 people, including of course the bulk of Herero women and children. Nor did the deaths of at least 30,000 Boers and 50,000 Africans in British camps during the Boer War of 1899–1902 occupy the attention of those committed to the Congo Reform Movement, any more than the Northern Nigeria campaign in which British General Lugard ordered the annihilation of the entire population of the town of Satiru, resulting in the deaths of thousands. It was left to the international socialist movement to reject colonialism in general, with socialists given the task of especially opposing the colonialism of their own nation.

In 1896, at the Third Congress of the Second International, a resolution was passed in which it was stated that "whatever the pretext, whether it be religious or in the interests of so-called civilization colonial extension is only another name for the extension of the area of capitalist exploitation in the exclusive interests of the capitalist class." Later congresses would call for unity with all those native peoples resisting colonialism and for workers to use "all means at their disposal to combat colonial expansion." The British socialist H. M. Hyndman, speaking of British rule in India, would call for the condemnation of "the British government for having destroyed a civilization which was perhaps better than ours" (*The International Working Class Movement*, vol. 2, 528). At the next Congress, held in Paris in 1900, charging Britain with creating famine in India by importing cheap Indian grain while tens of millions perished from hunger, Hyndman called for an uprising of the Indian people against British rule. The Indian delegate to the Congress, Dadhabhai Naoroji, received a standing ovation when he rose to speak to the Congress. Nor were the positions of the socialists all merely paper declarations. It was the socialist Ledebour who smuggled a copy of General von Trotha's extermination proclamation to the Herero people into the Reichstag, where he read it aloud, sending German politics into a crisis. A decade later, socialists in the so-called Red Belt of Northern Italy launched an all-out assault against the colonial wars in Africa, sabotaging train tracks and burning railway stations to stop the movement of troops and ammunition, blockading roads, and undertaking regional general strikes.

Conrad, an arch-conservative, followed the rise and development of socialism with a kind of horrified fascination. He would even become close friends in the 1890s with Cunninghame Graham, a flamboyant figure who was both a socialist and a Scottish nobleman (it was the latter quality, as Conrad repeatedly said, that allowed the two to become friends). A little more than ten years before the composition of *Heart of Darkness*, Conrad wrote a letter of which the rhetoric and terminology connects it closely with the apocalyptic tone of the latter text. Enraged by the passage of an electoral reform bill in the British parliament that doubled the number of voters, in effect enfranchising the previously disenfranchised working class, Conrad declares inevitable the emergence of working-class parties (and he was right: the Labour Party came into being within a few years) and the concomitant growth of socialism:

> the International Socialist Association are triumphant, and every disreputable ragamuffin in Europe feels that the day of universal brotherhood, dispoilation and disorder is coming apace, and nurses day-dreams of well-plenished pockets amongst the ruin of all that is respectable, venerable and holy. The great British Empire went over the edge, and yet on the inclined plane of social progress and radical reform. The downward movement is hardly perceptible yet, and the clever men who started it may flatter themselves with the progress; but they will soon find the fate of the nation is out of their hands now! The alpine avalanche rolls quicker and quicker as it nears the abyss – its ultimate destination! . . . England was the only barrier to the pressure of infernal doctrines born in continental back-slums. Now there is nothing!

Brotherhood, despoilation and disorder: Kurtz then is the perfect embodiment of socialism and the labor movement as Conrad saw it. Its ideals, the ideals of brotherhood and the redistribution of wealth, were nothing more than a cover for the ambitions of a few leaders. In the same letter, he would write that "socialism must invariably end in Caesarism" or Kurtzism. There is no radicalism, only human greed attempting to disguise itself: despoilation is coming apace, Europe nears the abyss of barbarism and criminality.

The murmur of the crowds becomes intermingled with the sounds of water and wind, of irresistible, uncontrollable natural forces. And just as the murmurs of the crowds disrupt and fragment the Intended's discourse at the conclusion of Marlow's narrative, so a voice murmurs over and through *Heart of Darkness,* interrupting it, preventing it from closing upon itself in completion, opening it to other texts, other histories. The voice is not the whine of those pleading the "right of labor to live"; it is the voice of the living power of labor, the power of cannibal crews, armed savages, mutineers and the apocalyptic moment of the mass strike. It is a voice in which can no longer be distinguished the chants of savages and the chants of

200,000 workers on May Day, the mutinous sailors' cry of protest and the incomprehensible words cried from afar, the expression of a power that threatens to bring about the ruin of all that is respectable, venerable and holy and cast civilization itself into the abyss. Between 1899 and 1917, this power would increase exponentially; assembled together in ever larger numbers to enrich or defend, in factories and armies, the interests of "their" civilization, masses would, as Conrad feared, explode into action: strikes, mutinies and finally revolution would follow: 1917 was the crucial year when millions of men and women, North and South, East and West, came to the conclusion that the only savages were those in Washington, London, Paris and Berlin. Even, as we have noted, the text of *Heart of Darkness* would not remain untouched: the word "wild" would disappear into the crowds of workers, soldiers and sailors as they set out to cast imperialism into the abyss. They failed, of course, allowing the civilized to inflict on the world, horrors which even Conrad could never have imagined.

Robinson Crusoe and the drama of interpellation

For decades, Defoe scholars have rebuked readers, even in academia, for having confused the "myth of Robinson Crusoe" with the literary work. The myth of Robinson Crusoe, now more than two centuries old, consists of a theoretical and political doctrine abstracted from the novel. It provides an illustration of individualism whether considered as an analytical approach to society or as a prescriptive political doctrine. The two individualist projects often work together, the analytical approach serving as the conceptual foundation for the norms of liberal or neo-liberal thought. Thus, it is not at all uncommon to see an argument for the reduction of society to market relations (individuals exchanging with other individuals motivated by self-interest alone), supported with a reference to a methodological individualism in which Robinson Crusoe, with or without Friday, is called upon to enact certain of the axioms governing the individual's maximization of utilities.

Literary specialists hasten to inform us that such notions, whatever their validity as propositions about the world, cannot help us read the text and, further, can only be sustained as readings of the text by suppressing its historical context in general and Defoe's place in it in particular, his other works, his beliefs, his activities. The historical context as they see it and the peculiarities of Defoe's life compel us, in contrast, to situate the novel in the tradition of the spiritual autobiography, a narrative of one individual's fall and subsequent redemption, the retracing of the steps of his spiritual progress from youth to the novel's present, Crusoe's old age. His island solitude and all that pertains to it, must be seen as a moment, even if prolonged, in the progress of God's providence and Crusoe's recognition of his place therein. It is this very providence that requires Crusoe to report even the most seemingly insignificant details of his material life and which necessitates the development of a realistic style: the greatness of God's design imposes meaning and purpose on all that exists and all that occurs. To extract a moment from this process and view it in isolation, and, even more, to transform it into a myth (Marx even gave such myths the generic name of "Robinsonades") is to fail to understand both the narrative in its totality and the ideology of dissenting Protestantism that informs it.

We seem thus to be confronted with two mutually exclusive interpretations: *Robinson Crusoe* would appear to resemble one of those images in which the observer will discern either a rabbit or a duck, depending upon the perspective from which the figure is viewed. The novel can be read as an epic of individualism, even possessive individualism, in which the world, "bathed in light" as Marx remarked, is a material world waiting to be appropriated and transformed by human labor. It is a world bereft of any original meaning, little more than brute matter to be shaped according to human design. Crusoe's island is, then, the state of nature imagined by early liberal philosophers, especially Hobbes and Locke, that is, the human condition before originally separate and dissociated individuals agree by mutual consent (the famous social contract) to unite under and transfer their right of self-government to, the state. At the same time, *Robinson Crusoe* may be read as a narrative not of the world's materiality, but of the necessity of transcending the natural to discover the meaning and purpose God has assigned to all creatures great and small, to every element in his creation. Crusoe's solitude would form a necessary means to this end, his removal from civilized society a deliverance from its temptations, a chance to will what God has in fact planned for him, namely his re-birth. According to this perspective, he will return like the Prodigal Son to the community he once willingly abandoned.

For each reading, the other mistakes the inessential for the essential in the narrative and posits a meaning to which the text must be reduced by the act of interpretation itself: either religion is a function of the social and political nature of the novel or social and political elements are mere moments in the progress of Crusoe's soul, moments whose significance is conferred by the providential design of the whole. Further, these alternatives appear to reproduce in the form of an interpretive dilemma, the central conflict of the eighteenth century, the struggle between faith and reason, or between enlightenment and superstition. If, however, we insist on the materiality of the text, we must cease to regard the counterposed readings of *Robinson Crusoe* as mere interpretations, that is, as subjective acts on the part of diverse readers, and instead ask in what way they are determined by the text itself. If we are not to ignore the way that our reading is never innocent, but is as historically determined as the work itself, we must begin our inquiry by acknowledging the interpretive alternatives that are imposed on us.

I will start by examining two passages that have a particular bearing on the interpretive controversy surrounding *Robinson Crusoe*. The first concerns the "will" and "commands" of Crusoe's father. Retracing the steps of his life from the vantage point of old age and discerning in every moment a meaning and direction invisible to him as he lived it, Crusoe maintains that his decision to disobey his father and ignore his commands against his son's going to sea was not the exercise of his free will or an assertion of his autonomy. On the contrary, an "inclination" (a term whose meaning in Defoe's time was closer to "instinct" than it is today) led him "strongly against the will, nay, the commands" of his father. In fact, "there seemed to be something fatal in that propension of nature tending directly to the life of misery which was to befal me." Crusoe is driven internally by a propensity that is in turn the correlate of external fate, his destiny. He could not avoid choosing a preordained course of action that would "tend directly" to years of penitential exile, followed by a redemptive homecoming and reconciliation. What then is the precise nature of his father's will and commands, the disregarding of which will bring upon him so much misery?

> My father, a wise and grave man, gave me serious and excellent counsel against what he foresaw was my design. . . . He asked me what reasons more than a mere wandering inclination I had for leaving my father's house and my native country, where I might be well introduced and had a prospect of raising my fortune by applica-

> tion and industry, with a life of ease and pleasure. He told me it was for men of desperate Fortunes on the one hand, or of aspiring, superior fortunes on the other, who went abroad upon adventures, to rise by enterprise and make themselves famous in undertakings out of the common road. (Defoe 1965, 27–8)

Finally, his father will conclude his discourse with a statement which Crusoe tells us was

> truly prophetick, tho' I suppose my father did not know it to be so himself: he would venture to say to me that if I did take this foolish step, God would not bless me and I would have leisure hereafter to reflect upon having neglected his counsel when there might be none to assist in my recovery. (Ibid., 28)

Crusoe's father's speech is crucial to the narrative; not only does it link paternal authority to that of God, so that the violation of the father's commands will incur God's wrath, it underscores the coincidence of the content of his father's commands and God's will. Crusoe is thus born neither to freedom nor equality, at least according to the doctrines of his father; rather, he is born into the family, a fact that confers obligations and duties upon him from the start. In particular, he is born in a state of subjection to his father's authority, given that the family is a hierarchically organized natural community whose existence derives from the will of God. We might go even further and say that an individual's place socially and geographically, far from deriving from an accident of birth, is assigned to him by nature, which is itself organized according to divine providence. Accordingly, Crusoe's father's doctrine is one of social immobility; Crusoe should leave neither his father's house nor his native land, nor should he attempt to "rise by enterprize" beyond the rank into which he was born. Felicity will consist of rising only within one's station, not beyond it. To attempt to rise too far is to risk falling below, to the station of mere "mechanicks" or laborers. His father's words are indeed prophetic from this perspective: Crusoe, deprived of all society on the island, will experience to the fullest the terrifying void of "freedom," freedom from father, family, nation in which, without the support of others, he will be forced to live by the sweat of his brow. He will be compelled as best he can to reinvent and recreate all that would have been offered to him had he remained in his father's house, and to live without fellowship of any kind (until, after many years, Friday is delivered to him). Further, his father's speech identifies the precepts or commandments that Crusoe will violate, thus simultaneously incurring punishment and establishing the possibility, through penance, of redemption.

Crusoe's account of his father's statement of both the form and the content of Crusoe's transgression and thus, also, his "punishment," however, is preceded by a brief history of his father's life that calls radically into question all the positions he attributes to his father. The novel begins:

> I was born in the year 1632, in the city of York, of a good family, tho' not of that country, my father being a foreigner of Bremen, who settled first at Hull. He got a good estate by merchandise, and leaving off his trade lived afterward at York, from whence he married my mother, whose relations were named Robinson, a very good family in that country from whom I was called Robinson Kreutznaer; but by the usual corruption of words in England, we are now called, nay we call ourselves and write our name, Crusoe, and so my companions always called me. (Ibid., 27)

When we place the two passages side by side, the effect is quite jarring. Crusoe's father not only did all the things he warns his son not to do, but instead of being punished for "leaving his father's house and native country," he earns sufficient money to retire and raise a family (significantly, like Robinson Crusoe, at a very advanced age). We are informed that his father left Bremen, but there is no mention whatever of his family, who make no appearance in the novel at all. Further, the father earns and therefore does not arrive with the fortune that alone according to the father's advice to Crusoe permits a man to go abroad to seek his fortunes. In a very important sense, Crusoe's wandering inclination is nothing more than a repetition of the father's own (successful) actions, which themselves speak louder than his words. Perhaps most interesting of all, however, is that not only the foreignness of the family name, but the father's family and his separation from them are obscured by the anglicization of Kreutznaer to Crusoe, which permits a forgetting of family and nation. We might go further and say that the modification of the name also conceals the dissociation and mobility that preceded what the father seeks to present as nature: Crusoe's father's house, his fortune, are a consequence of his leaving not remaining in his father's house, under his authority. The stability of family and society do not exist by nature, they are made, produced by human labor and then offered as nature. The world, social as well as natural, is and has always been in perpetual motion. The father moves from one port city, Bremen, to another, Hull, following the circuit of trade, just as Crusoe will move between Europe, Guinea and the Brazils.

Thus, *Robinson Crusoe* begins not simply in a moment of stark contradiction, but in full dissociation: nowhere does Crusoe acknowledge the discrepancy that he himself communicates between his father's actions and his words, between his practice and his morality. The text simply exhibits without in any way attempting to overcome or even address this conflict. It is no wonder then that the work has produced such divergent and opposed interpretations; they are the direct effect of the irreconcilably antagonistic meanings present from the first page. Do these meanings, linked as they are to opposing political doctrines, simply lead a peaceful coexistence in the novel, each developing independently of the other without interference, to such a degree that readers can follow one trajectory through the course of the narrative without ever encountering the other? On the contrary, it would appear that the discrepancy that emerges around the father, once registered, produces certain specific effects. The very doctrine to which the father appeals in his discourse with his son, the doctrine of individuals born into the community of the family and therefore under the authority of the father, of a larger social hierarchy fixed by nature and by Providence, in retrospect appears as nothing more than a myth designed by those who have risked and gained fortunes, in order to secure their advantage and their wish to obscure their origins. In reality, the son follows in the disavowed and denied footsteps of the father, who effortlessly left the family and the natural bonds it offered, easily abandoning his father's house and native land, the place allotted to him by Providence. Behind the façade of stability, then, change; behind the appearance of nature (itself the expression of God's will), human practice.

A few pages later, the first sign of God's displeasure with Crusoe, the storm that greets his first "ill-fated" voyage, is quickly revealed not to have been a storm at all, and therefore not a sign:

> The ship was no sooner gotten out of the Humber, but the wind began to blow and the waves to rise in a most frightful manner; and

> as I had never been at sea before, I was most inexpressibly sick in body and terrify'd in my mind. I began now seriously to reflect upon what I had done and how justly I was overtaken by the judgement of heaven for my wicked leaving my father's house, and abandoning all my duty. (Ibid., 31)

The next day, when Crusoe speaks to an experienced sailor of the storm of the previous night he is laughed at and called a fool for taking what was "but a capful of wind" for a storm. Thus, the attribution of supernatural meanings to natural events is revealed to be the consequence of an individual's ignorance (of the natural causes of natural events, and the frequency and regularity of these events), together with fear, that leads to the need to find an intention behind the apparently random workings of nature, or more precisely a God who being moved to act upon nature as his instrument can be induced to act otherwise by the entreaties and conduct of the individual who has displeased him. The development of the narrative, then, simultaneously offers a vision of Providence and the place of nature and humanity in it, and not only a vision of a purely natural world without supernatural causes, but a vision that constitutes a trenchant critique of any notion of an original order whether natural or human. In a certain sense Defoe represents the inversion of Pascal's notion of *Deus absconditus*: the notion that God had abandoned the world leaving behind the infinite void of His absence. While for Pascal the openness of the world was an abyss, there emerges in *Robinson Crusoe* (within and against the spiritual autobiography) a sense of unlimited freedom, of spaces waiting to be appropriated and made productive. Even absence in Crusoe's world takes on a positive significance: it is the absence of fixed places and identities, the absence of impediments to movement.

No concept is perhaps more important to either of the two opposing positions that so strikingly emerge in the first few pages of *Robinson Crusoe* than that of human sociability. There is nothing remarkable in this fact: the question of whether man was indeed the social animal described by Aristotle in his *Politics*, the animal whose physical nature, let alone intellectual inclinations, required that he live in a community, bound to his fellows by ties of love and friendship, occupied many of Defoe's contemporaries. Defoe's time, in fact, saw some of the most important and powerful challenges to the Aristotelian position on human sociability in the history of philosophy: Descartes's *Meditations*, Hobbes's *Leviathan*, and Locke's *Two*

Treatises of Government. Does society exist by nature as the element in which what is properly human, language, knowledge, culture must necessarily exist and outside of which an individual cannot be truly human but instead must sink to the level of a beast? Or, conversely, are individuals born free, not only free of any relations of authority and subordination, but fundamentally free or separate from others, with whom each one enters into social relations only by means of the artifice of a contract?

In fact, *Robinson Crusoe* appeals simultaneously to both positions. The very meaning of the island in the teleology of Crusoe's life is as a place of punishment (and penitence). When he draws a balance sheet of his experience shortly after arriving on the island, he lists as among the evils that have befallen him his solitude: "I am singled out and separated, as it were, from all the world to be miserable. . . . I am divided from mankind, a solitaire, one banished from humane society. . . . I have no soul to speak to or relieve me" (ibid., 83–4). This solitude, however, will prove to be his salvation, according to his own testimony, allowing or perhaps compelling him to turn away from the distractions of worldly life and contemplate eternal truths, to pass beyond appearances to the truth to which he was before blind: the workings of God's providence, which cast him on a barren island for the purpose of saving him. Even this strain in the novel is, however, interrupted by contradiction, a contradiction that can easily be derived from the popular reception of the novel. There is a sense, absolutely opposed to the first, in which Crusoe's solitude is not a punishment at all but the source of felicity, a felicity, moreover, which has nothing to do with providence. Crusoe discovers that solitude, far from being the miserable state he initially feared, is the state most suited to his nature, and that the presence of others brings not relief but anxiety and fear. In other words, Crusoe has discovered the state of nature as understood by early liberal philosophy, that original condition of autonomous individuals, born not only free of and equal to others, but (in theory, of course) separate, sharing neither interest nor desire. Every man is an island: Crusoe's island is the recovery of his autonomy in the face of the claims of family and community, those collectivities always ready to usurp the prerogatives of the individual. As he finishes his fourth year on the island, he tells us,

> I looked now upon the world as a thing remote, which I had nothing to do with, no expectation from, and indeed no desires about, in a

> word, I had nothing to do with it, nor was ever like to have; so I thought it looked as we may perhaps look upon it hereafter, viz., as a place I had lived in, but was come out of it. . . . In the first place, I was removed from all the wickedness of the world here. I had neither the lust of the flesh, the lust of the eye, or the pride of life. I had nothing to covet; for I had all that I was capable of enjoying; I was lord of the whole manor; or if I pleased, I might call myself king or emperor over the whole country which I had possession of. There were no rivals; I had no competitor, none to dispute sovereignty or command with me. (Ibid., 139)

There is then no social inclination, no natural impulse to participate in a community; it appears instead that Crusoe has discovered his essential aversion to others, whose presence necessarily threatens the autonomy and separateness that alone will bring him contentment. In a strangely elliptical figure, Crusoe refers to the "lust of the flesh." Women, present only at the margins of the novel (his mother, the widow), assume a maternal function. The presence of a woman in Crusoe's life in any other capacity would disrupt and call into question his separateness from others, as well as his self-government and self-ownership, by arousing an intense need to unite with another, a need regarded by Aristotle as the surest sign of human sociability. Crusoe's giving thanks for his delivery from the lust of the flesh calls attention to another related and similarly elliptical passage near the end of the work. In a parenthetical phrase contained in a long sentence six paragraphs before the conclusion of the narrative, Robinson Crusoe discloses his marriage and the subsequent death of his wife:

> In the mean time I in part settled myself here; for first of all I marry'd, and that not either to my disadvantage or dissatisfaction, and had three children, two sons and one daughter; but my wife dying, and my nephew coming home with good success from a voyage to Spain, my inclination to go abroad and his importunity, prevailed and engaged me to go in his ship, as a private trader to the East Indies. (Ibid., 298)

There are a number of elements here that deserve some scrutiny. First, Crusoe does not mention his marriage for its own sake, but rather to explain his remaining in England for a period of seven years after his return from the island. Defoe thus inverts the usual order of importance, relegating love and sexuality to the level of the incidental.

Crusoe's matrimony does not even constitute the topic of the sentence and the noun "wife" only appears at the moment he reports her death. Further, the advantages of their marriage are expressed in the double negative: the marriage was not to his disadvantage or dissatisfaction. The negative of "disadvantage," we assume, refers to the financial benefits he accrued from the alliance. The reference to the absence of "dissatisfaction" which follows, implies some sort of pleasure; that this pleasure is sexual may be concluded from the report immediately following the description of the marriage, that he (not they: he is the subject of the verb) had three children. By the next clause, separated by a colon from the report of his taking a wife, she is dead. His wife then does not even occupy a complete sentence; her life and death take place in two subordinate clauses.

Coming at the end of a narrative whose concluding pages are notorious for piling extraneous incidents, one upon another, Crusoe's abbreviated account of his long delayed matrimony may be thought to be no more essential to the text than the account of Friday's encounter with a bear in the Pyrenees (which receives a far lengthier and more detailed treatment) or any number of other disconnected moments in an extremely episodic text. Marriage, and love more generally, however, differ from Crusoe's other adventures: love, as one eighteenth-century admirer of the novel remarked, has been thought "necessary to make a romance interesting. But *Robinson Crusoe*, though there is nothing of love in it, is one of the most interesting narratives that ever was written" (Beattie 1783, 566). In fact, the nature of Crusoe's discussion of his marriage serves only to highlight and make conspicuous the absence of love in the novel. And there is nothing incidental about this absence: on the contrary, it is central to Defoe's project.

Thus, in the state of nature that Crusoe celebrates in his reflection on his fourth year on the island, free from the arbitrary constraints and artificial social and political hierarchies (masquerading as nature), he may become emperor, king or lord (all of which derive from hereditary succession). All authority, then, no matter how it presents itself, is shown to be artificial, determined not by some natural order but by power and wealth (if the two can be dissociated). Property, however, is another matter altogether; while Crusoe is outside the jurisdiction of any legal system (the Caribs, according to the narrative, have no genuine culture, and as Cannibals, are by their actions, not by nature, determined as below the threshold of humanity), his right does not simply extend to the use of the island and its resources for survival. Rather, he has sole possession of the island, he is its rightful owner, a fact that gives him great pleasure, a pleasure that could only be tempered by the presence of others, who would necessarily become rivals and competitors. Property neither presupposes nor requires the social state with its legality: rather, property exists in the immediate relation between the individual and nature prior to any law. In fact, ownership, especially the individual's self-ownership, is the foundation of all legitimate authority, a theme central to every relationship between Crusoe and another individual (apart from the family into which he was born). Defoe, here as elsewhere, follows Locke very closely:

> Though the earth, and all the inferior creatures, be common to all men, yet every man has a property in his own person; this no body has a right to but himself. The labor of his body, and the work of his hands, we may say, are properly his. Whatsoever then he removes out of that state that nature hath provided and left it in, he hath mixed his labor with and joined to it something that is his own, and thereby makes it his property. . . . As much land as a man tills, plants, improves, cultivates, and can use the product of, so much is his property. (Locke 1980: 19)

Thus, we seem to have arrived at a reading of *Robinson Crusoe* that has restored to it the complexity and even incoherence proper to it, the incoherence of positions in conflict. Were we to stop our analysis here, we might say that the novel recapitulates the struggle of its time, the struggle for Enlightenment, even when the struggle takes place within the discourse of faith and the supernatural. Locke too, as Althusser noted, was forced to postulate a God not by the coercion of external authority but as a transcendental prop for his very empiricism (and we might well argue that God was every bit as necessary to his political thought, especially insofar as it depends on the concept of individual property in the state of nature). In this way the contradictions so exorbitantly displayed in *Robinson Crusoe*, far from rendering the work inferior or flawed would be the key to its historical importance. The struggle between patriarchalism and liberalism, between Providence and Freedom, between supernaturalism and naturalism, however, does not exhaust the antagonisms that traverse the novel. For if Defoe's text has functioned historically as one of the great statements, albeit in fictional form, of early liberalism despite the spiritual autobiography that it demonstrably contains, this element too is disfigured and discomposed insofar as the work, as Macherey put it, "is compelled to say more than it wants to say," or needs to say (Macherey 1978, 64).

We might begin with one of the novel's most memorable statements not only of individual self-sufficiency, but of equality:

> So I went to work; and here I must needs observe, that as reason is the substance and original of the mathematics, so by stating and squaring everything by reason, and by making the most rational judgement of things, every man may be in time master of every mechanick art. I had never handled a tool in my life, and yet in time, by labor, application, and contrivance, I found at last that I wanted nothing but I could have made it. (Defoe 1965, 85)

Every individual possesses sufficient reason to reinvent technical culture from zero. One needs no more than to apply oneself diligently, to exercise one's reason with care. In this sense, *Robinson Crusoe* is the literary analogue to Descartes's *Meditations*, the primary difference between them consisting in the fact that rather than negate existing culture through an act of will in order then to rebuild it on the solid foundations of reason alone, Crusoe's foundations are forcibly pulled out from under him, and he is left quite literally to swim in water too deep to stand in. His relation to his tools, his products, is henceforth unmediated by others. Whatever the initial inconvenience of his deprivation, his being compelled to rely on his own reason alone not only allows him quickly to compensate for the absence of society, but demonstrates that he, like all individuals, contains in him, in potential form, all that the previous history of technology has produced. Thus, given the appropriate circumstances, he is revealed to be the equal of any man, no matter how great his intelligence or how high his level of skill, and this equality furnishes the material basis for his autonomy, his separateness. Society thus emerges as superfluous or worse, a hindrance to one's full development with its artificial constraints and hierarchies, and its parade of temptations and distractions. If only Crusoe hadn't discovered that single footprint (the single footprint: not even a pair of feet, as if symptomatically Defoe has reduced even the biped to one, the individual beyond the irreducible minimum)!

In the most important sense, however, Crusoe has invented or discovered nothing by means of his own rationality. Moreover, he is by no means without the benefit of human society. On the contrary, he owes his survival to the labor, skill and intelligence of thousands of others whose work is incarnate and congealed in the ship and its stores. Not only does it supply the tools and materials necessary to the procurement of food and shelter, but it offers instruction in every "mechanic art" by illustrating the process of design and production of which the very nails of the ship are the result. Adam Smith, himself an admirer of *Robinson Crusoe*, would describe the way in which the clothes of the poorest laborer in England embody the combined labor of multitudes. In this sense, society has accompanied Robinson Crusoe into his island solitude, protecting him and giving him the tools, both manual and intellectual, necessary for his survival. The novel illustrates Spinoza's contention that no one ever exists outside of society, because society has no outside. Crusoe, however, takes no note of this fact, claiming to have discovered for himself what others, in fact a great many others, over a period of centuries, have provided for him. The notion of the autonomous, self-sufficient individual in a state of nature prior to or outside of society is thus itself revealed to be no more true than the patriarchalist doctrines it denounces as fiction. Early liberal theories of the state of nature become simply another form of denial, the denial of the social existence that alone makes the life of the individual possible.

A fiction or a denial: but to what end? It is here that Crusoe's relations with the few others who populate the vast spaces of Defoe's novel assume their full significance. The very notion of a pre-social state of nature in which individuals are absolutely separate and autonomous had a specifically political function for its proponents, notably Hobbes and Locke. If individuals are ordered by nature alone and therefore self-governing (perhaps because they are self-owning), any political order that does not reject nature and the natural rights which alone can furnish genuine political legitimacy, must be based on the voluntary transfer of the right to self-government, otherwise known as consent. The origin of legitimate government is then the contract into which all the individuals concerned have entered freely. In fact, the origin of every legitimate relation between individuals in which some exchange is involved must be contractual in origin. (After all, why would any individual labor for or give money to another except out of self-interest?) Early liberal philosophers could not agree on the family: was it an entirely contractual union in which the child has "tacitly" consented to obey and later support the parents in return for their care and support (which, after all, if so inclined, they might have withdrawn); or did there exist certain natural bonds of affection mandated perhaps by God's commandments, but in any case, absolutely distinct from political and social relations, which were necessarily contractual in origin?

We have noted that Robinson Crusoe tends to call into question the most common extra-economic social bonds: Defoe minimizes the importance of both the parent–child and sexual relation (the latter in fact is undertaken for "advantage"). What of the other relations in the novel? All but the most trivial are founded on a contract. One of the most instructive in this regard appears in the scene of his escape from Moorish slavery with his fellow slave, Xury. Having disposed of their guard while the two slaves are in their master's boat, Crusoe and Xury are suddenly cast into the state of nature as described by Locke, if not Hobbes. There exists no bond of solidarity or fellowship between two individuals who suffer their bondage in common; not even a utilitarian calculation of shared interest can be permitted to induce Crusoe to accept Xury without the mediation of a contract. Instead the two masterless individuals conclude a voluntary agreement according to whose terms Xury exchanges his freedom, his self-government, and self-ownership in return for Crusoe's refraining from destroying him. There remain, of course, certain inalienable rights: Xury is free to decline the offer and swim the mile or so to shore and take his chances there. Understandably, he chooses the former course and becomes Crusoe's servant, only to be sold by Crusoe to the captain of a Portuguese slave ship.

The encounter with Friday would similarly appear to be an example of free and equal individuals arriving at a relation through the mediation of a contract. The two men meet in a classic state of nature: there exists no legitimate authority over either individual and both are free to establish dominion over or subject themselves to the other. They are brought together by mutual self-interest. Friday is one of two captives of the Cannibals, who are preparing to devour him. Crusoe, now aging, desires a slave or "servant, and perhaps a companion or assistant," not so much to relieve his solitude, which, it should be recalled, he now quite enjoys, as to diminish the labor necessary to secure his comforts. After watching Friday escape his captors, Crusoe steps forward to "save this poor creature's life" and shoots and kills

Friday's two pursuers (Defoe 1965, 206). This is the moment of the contract, voluntarily concluded by reason of self-interest between the two men. Seeing "his enemies fallen and killed," Friday "was so frighted with the fire and noise of my piece, that he stood stock still and neither came forward or went backward":

> I beckoned him again to come to me and gave him all the signs of encouragement that I could think of, and he came nearer and nearer, kneeling down every ten or twelve steps in token of acknowledgement for my saving his life. I smiled at him and looked pleasantly, and beckoned to him to come nearer still; at length he kneeled down again, kissed the ground, and laid his head upon the ground, and, taking me by the foot, set my foot upon his head; this it seems was in token of swearing to be my slave for ever. (Ibid., 207)

In the guise of a portrayal of a voluntary contract concluded by free and equal individuals in the state of nature, this passage from *Robinson Crusoe* offers everything necessary for a critical analysis of this founding fiction of bourgeois society. In fact, a more salient image of "voluntary subjection" could hardly be imagined: an unarmed man "voluntarily" subjects himself to another man who happens to be standing over him with a loaded weapon. However equal they may be in the sight of God or in law, they are physically unequal: one man is capable instantly of killing the other, who is defenseless before him. In an almost allegorical form, this image captures the fundamental dissymmetry between formally equal individuals in the sphere of economic production. The worker, now free – that is, dispossessed of the land he might once have occupied and which furnished him with food, clothing and shelter or at least the means to procure the same – can survive only be earning a wage from those who possess the land or other means of production. He freely, voluntarily enters into the labor contract in the sense that no law directly compels him to do so: he is perfectly at liberty to choose homelessness and starvation if he so wills, in precisely the same way that Friday might have chosen to flee the armed stranger standing over him. To take the resemblance even further, should any dispute arise between worker and employer, the latter has at his disposal, as Adam Smith recognized, all the means of "legitimate," state violence, the police and army.

Crusoe and the savage kneeling before him (soon to be named

Friday) do not speak the same language; they do not even share a lexicon of gestures or signs. We are therefore confronted with a scene that consists of two individuals making mutually unintelligible gestures in utter silence. In the face of this unintelligible corporeality, Crusoe engages in a hermeneutic operation which discovers behind the disposition of the body, behind incomprehensible sounds, the idea that lies at the origin. "It seems" that the intention behind Friday's action was to signal that he "swore to be Crusoe's slave for life." This discovery is far from incidental: the only thing that legitimizes Crusoe's power over the savage and that differentiates his subjection of Friday from that of his previous "owners" is the act of will invisible except in the bodily movements that are its apparent expression. It would be difficult to imagine a more fitting illustration of Althusser's phrase: "the individual is interpellated as a (free) subject in order that he shall submit freely to the commands of the Subject, i.e., in order that he shall (freely) accept his subjection" (Althusser 1971, 182).

Even this cursory reading of *Robinson Crusoe* reveals that far from gathering itself into a coherent whole as it proceeds from beginning to end, the text progresses through a dissociative movement the force of which pulls it apart, separating it from itself. This dissociation, however, is not the effect of some primal disorder or indeterminacy; it is historically determined by the multiple and intersecting struggles of Defoe's time: not simply the struggle of citizen against state, but also the propertyless against the propertied, worker against employer, slave against master. Perhaps, then, it is possible to read the sense of openness we find in *Robinson Crusoe* as something more than the openness of a world offering itself up for capitalist appropriation: might it not be the openness of a history without end, not even the end of the universalization of capital; the openness of a world to be made?

The Future Lasts Forever: Althusser after Althusser

In 1976, Althusser would sum up in a single epigram from Marx what he called "the golden rule of materialism: do not judge a being by its self consciousness. Every being is other than its self consciousness" (Althusser 1996b, 115). Less than 10 years later, Althusser would violate this rule in the most flagrant of ways: he would write an autobiography entitled *The Future Lasts Forever* (*L'Avenir dure longtemps*), in which he attempts, without a trace of irony or self-consciousness, to explain how he became what he is (and why he has done what he has done), granting all the privileges usually accorded to one's intimate (that is, unmediated and direct) knowledge of oneself. After all, common sense (the very common sense that Althusser elsewhere asked us unmercifully to interrogate) tells us that no one else knows us as we know ourselves, that no one can know because no one has access to the internal world beyond or behind the physicality of our bodily actions, including that of the voice that speaks or the hand that writes. No one can know the thoughts and feelings which are not expressed in some form and which thus remain private, invisible and inaudible, enclosed in our heart of hearts. An autobiography, then, would be the privileged expression of this hidden realm.

The fact that this is precisely the philosophy of consciousness against which not only Althusser but the contemporaries he regarded as his philosophical allies (Lacan, Foucault, Deleuze and Derrida) directed their major works in no way prevents him from writing a late twentieth-century version of what he invokes as his model: Rousseau's *Confessions.* Althusser tells us near the beginning of *The Future*,

> I can in all honesty subscribe to the following declaration of his: "I shall say openly what I did, what I thought, what I was." I would simply add: "what I understood or believed I understood, what I no longer altogether control (more literally, 'that of which I am no longer completely master' [*ce dont je ne suis plus tout à fait le maître*]) but what I have become." (Althusser 1992: 29)

To Rousseau's promise of honesty, the promise to say everything, whether thoughts or actions, no matter how embarrassing or shameful they may be, Althusser adds the attempt to understand, even if, he admits in a gesture of humility, the understanding he adds to the raw data of his life may not really be understanding, but only what he believes, perhaps wrongly, he has understood. His narrative, as he himself describes it at the outset of the work, is not fundamentally different from the narrative of *Robinson Crusoe*: "I shall sometimes describe things in the order in which they happened and sometimes anticipate or recall certain moments" (ibid., 29). It is this order – not strictly an evolutionary succession but a time in which the past already contains the future and the future the past – in which similitude unfolds in the guise of change. It is the process which, he tells us, "made me what I am" (ibid., 29). Althusser's life as he narrates it has a beginning, a middle and an end. It is this end, which Althusser survived in order to describe, that constitutes in every imaginable way the autobiography's purpose. It is also that act to which all the steps of which his life consists, insensibly led him (if he is to be believed), the act which determined that he would no longer be his own master: the act by which, in 1980, he strangled his wife Hélène Legotien.

We have noted that one of Althusser's most productive theoretical contributions was his argument that individuals are interpellated, that is, hailed or addressed, as subjects (authors and owners of their own words and deeds) by Ideological State Apparatuses (ISAs). Althusser furnishes the example (which I suggested earlier might well have been inspired by Beckett's *Molloy*) of "the most banal form of hailing by the police (or others): 'Hey, you there!'" This hailing, as we saw in the case of *Molloy*, and as we know from everyday life, is but the prelude to an interrogation during which the interpellated subject will be called upon to answer for himself: What is your name, what are you doing here, where are you going? It is thus not only the act of interpellation that "constitutes" the individual as subject, but his response to the addresses of the ISAs. Most individuals affirm themselves as subjects by answering the call; they become subjects by subjecting themselves. They speak and act as free agents because they have been called upon to do so and not simply in the case of being stopped by a policeman: they have always already been called upon to answer for themselves. Most people, in fact, are the subjected subjects that Althusser describes and as such, he tells us, "work all by themselves," never requiring the addresses of a policeman, "freely" subjecting themselves to the authority incarnate in law and work. There exist, however, those exceptional "bad subjects" who require the intervention not of the ISAs but of the Repressive State Apparatus: the police, the courts, the prisons. But even they (or perhaps, especially they) remain subjects, addressed as the authors of the acts for which they must assume responsibility and for which they are liable to penalties and punishments.

The Future Lasts Forever, interestingly, not only resists the schema sketched out above, but reveals another dimension of the interpellation of subjects (whether good subjects who willingly answer when they are called or bad subjects who refuse to answer a summons).

Although Althusser took the life of another person, as he tells us in the very first sentence of the text, he was declared unfit to plead or to stand trial for his action by reason of insanity. His decades-long history of mental illness and his increasingly frequent and prolonged delusional states, hitherto known only to a restricted circle of friends, became public knowledge. He was thus judged or interpellated neither as a good subject (who committed a bad act but involuntarily and who will assume responsibility only for that portion of the act to which he actively consented) nor as a bad subject (who intentionally committed a crime, in this case, murder). Instead, he became a madman, incapable of assuming the position of a subject at all, neither responsible for the act he committed nor capable of assuming responsibility for any words that he might utter. To be judged insane, then, is to cease to be a subject at all; not only does one cease to be held accountable for one's actions, but more importantly, the actions and words of the person judged insane are deprived of meaning. Perhaps nothing in Foucault's *Madness and Civilization* so fascinated Althusser as the idea that the "Almost general and concrete" definition of madness or insanity (*folie*), which only emerged a few centuries ago as the other of Reason, was the *absence d'oeuvre*, the absence of work (as in a work of art). What does this phrase, so difficult to translate, mean? Behind the actions and words of the madman lies an absence of meaning. His actions, then, are not properly actions at all insofar as actions are understood as fulfilling a pre-existing intention; they are, rather, disconnected movements, indistinguishable from bodily tremors or the movement of limbs during a seizure, without prior purpose or design. Similarly, his speech does not consist of words at all; it is mere noise, the bearer not of meaning but of nonsense. According to Foucault, madness is that against which reason measures itself, the absence of meaning in relation to which reason defines itself as meaningful and purposive. Indeed, Althusser paid homage to Foucault when he announced that the project of *Reading Capital* was inscribed in the history of reason that Foucault's work was meant to inaugurate, reason in its struggle against unreason, meaning against nonsense:

> However paradoxical it may seem, I venture to suggest that our age threatens one day to appear in the history of human culture as marked by the most dramatic and difficult trial of all, the discovery and training in the meaning of the "simplest" acts of existence:

> seeing, listening, speaking, reading – the acts which relate men to their works and to those works thrown in their faces, their "absences of works." (Althusser 1996a, 15–16)

This memorable passage describes the opening of a problematic in which the relation of the author to work is not only not direct and unmediated, but subject to historical variation and haunted by the absence of works, by the absence of meaning.

The third sentence of *The Future* clearly situates the work in what Althusser elsewhere calls the drama of interpellation: "This book is that response which I would otherwise have been compelled to give. And all I ask is that I be allowed to give it, that I be allowed now to do what would otherwise have been an obligation" (Althusser 1992,13). Althusser forces us to rethink the nature of this drama and to recognize that its players are not simply those called upon to speak and act as subjects, or rather who are deemed responsible (causally as well as legally) for certain actions and discourses, but also those who cannot be subjects and whose actions and discourse, if they can be said to be theirs at all, are never "works" in Foucault's sense, but precisely movements and sounds that resist the imprint of meaning. The autobiography is, then, written in the past perfect tense, the counterfactual testimony Althusser "would have given" had he been compelled by the law to do so. The psychoanalytic commentaries on Althusser's text (it immediately elicited a number of such commentaries and we should regard this fact as an objective effect of the text itself, but also a lure or decoy in Lacan's sense, an element that works to divert our attention from other elements) have neglected the fact that far from resembling a set of associations from which the meaning of Althusser's act might be reconstructed, it is structured as testimony and governed by the logic of what has a bearing on his "case." Because everything is designed to explain the act by which he took the life of another person, those facts that are irrelevant are omitted. Other aspects of his life, such as his philosophical work, which might have been regarded as immaterial to the disposition of the case are reinterpreted in such a way as to make them relevant to the testimony that Althusser would have given had he been compelled to do so. It is precisely the juridical context of *The Future*, however imaginary this context might be, that dictates its form, its attempt to reconstruct for purposes of evaluation the criminal's "state of mind" before and during the commission of the crime. "No one before me has made such a critical confession," writes Althusser (ibid., 29).

All that Foucault has written about the ritual of confession applies to Althusser's narrative: the motif of confession grants the individual unique access to the truth of his own being. Of course, the one who confesses may require guidance and support in his quest to know himself and to transmit that knowledge in the form of spoken or written discourse, or, conversely, he may require external inducements, persuasion or even coercion before he communicates the privileged knowledge of himself that he alone possesses. Confession always

> unfolds within a power relationship, for one does not confess without the presence (or virtual presence) of a partner who is not simply the interlocutor but the authority who requires the confession, prescribes and appreciates it, and intervenes in order to judge, punish, forgive, console, and reconcile; a ritual in which truth is corroborated by the obstacles and resistances it has had to surmount in order to be formulated. (Foucault 1978, 61–2)

At first, it appears that the obstacles and resistances are external to Althusser: not only has he been denied by the Repressive State Apparatus the opportunity to explain himself, and legally reduced to a man "sans oeuvre," whose words are no longer regarded as juridically meaningful, but his close friends, he tells us, advised him not to attempt to explain what happened and why, fearing that any statement by Althusser, especially any lucid statement, would provoke a reaction from the public that might lead to more repressive measures against him. A lengthy and well-organized confession might convey the impression that Althusser never was insane, that he adopted the "insanity defense" as a way of avoiding prison. However well intentioned these unnamed friends are, Althusser argues, they too have helped to silence him, to bury him "under a tombstone of silence" to cite the phrase he repeatedly uses (Althusser 1992, 22).

But of course there are also internal obstacles: the feelings of guilt and shame he must overcome fully to explain what he has become. The book begins, jarringly, after a very brief prefatory statement, with a detailed reconstruction of the strangulation of Hélène Legotien and its immediate aftermath, a scene which concludes with Althusser succumbing to an injection of a sedative and sinking into oblivion. He has recounted, he tells us, "my precise memory of those events forever engraved in my mind through all my suffering" (ibid., 15). But the bringing to light of this horrifying scene, the verbalization of or the giving of order to what might have remained an inchoate set of disconnected images, is merely the first in a series of thoughts, desires and memories once hidden (not just from others, but perhaps even from himself), now pronounced out loud, written down, and from that moment beyond his control, for all to see and to make of what they will. He tells us the secrets of his youth, his fears and lifelong cowardice, but also his longings and sexual desires; he will violate the prohibitions of polite and scholarly discourse to speak of things such as nocturnal emissions and masturbation. He describes his long relationship with Hélène, overcoming considerable discomfort to recall the suffering he inflicted on her with his affairs with other women, some carried on openly as if to provoke her. His portrait of her is an idealizing one. "Others" may have thought her (and him) impossible, but they did not really know her, her intelligence, her empathy. She was the embodiment of the labor of the negative, of a suffering so great that it could not be expressed in words but only written in the wrinkles and creases of her skin, in the posture of a body perpetually clenched as if in anticipation of blows.

If these admissions no longer quite possess the shock value they might once have had, Althusser holds in reserve others that, while less offensive to public decency, may bring upon him more opprobrium. He tells us, with apparent sincerity, that he has been an intellectual fraud from the moment he entered the Lycée. There, Althusser confesses, he learned the art of writing beautiful sounding and convincing essays on topics of which he was entirely ignorant. He seeks to convince the reader that from the beginning to the end of his career he succeeded in academia through deception and imposture. Naturally, it is shocking to read that the head of the philosophy program at France's most prestigious and exclusive university, and indeed a philosopher of international renown whose works have been translated into more than twenty languages, knew very little philosophy: while, according to his testimony, he knew Pascal and Descartes well and Malebranche tolerably well, his readers will undoubtedly be surprised to learn that, by mid-career, he knew only a little Hegel, Spinoza and Rousseau and, moreover, that he never understood a word of Freud or Lacan. Let us, for the moment, leave to the side the demonstrable falsity of these last "confessions." After all, as Althusser argues at another point in the narrative, "Hallucinations are also facts" (ibid., 81). It does not really matter that many of the confessions may be false; Althusser must still struggle against shame and anxiety to make public what he fears and perhaps even at moments believes is true. Fantasies produce real effects.

At this point, we are forced to pose an obvious question: did Althusser in his last phase renounce the theoretical anti-humanism that, as we saw earlier, was not only the notion most associated with him (by critics and admirers alike), but was the concept in his work that most affected the theoretical and political conjuncture he inhabited? How else might we understand a phrase like the following, which occurs near the end of the narrative: "all I seek to do is to elucidate if possible the deep-seated personal motives, both conscious and especially unconscious which underpinned" his entire academic and political career (ibid., 169). He vows on a number of occasions to "illuminate" or to "say out loud" what has remained unknown or unspoken, not only to others but to himself. We are clearly far from the notion of the unconscious which Althusser hailed as the great discovery of psychoanalysis in his essay "Freud and Lacan." There he speaks of the paradox of an irreducibly double discourse of the signifying chain between whose divergent meanings the subject is condemned infinitely to oscillate, of the unconscious as described by Lacan, the discourse of an Other who speaks only where I am not (Lacan 1977, 17–21). The notion of the unconscious invoked in *The Future,* in contrast, is closer to the concept definitively excluded by Lacan's work, a concept of the unconscious as a place in us, difficult of access to be sure and surrounded, as it were, by formidable defenses, but ultimately penetrable by those possessed of sufficient fortitude and guided by the proper spirit. This second notion of the unconscious as a subconscious is, as Lacan repeatedly said, Cartesian rather than Freudian. According to this view, the division of the subject is the source of its neurotic misery and must be overcome for the subject to gain control over and take responsibility for itself. Has Althusser returned to such a conception in opposition to what he himself repeatedly argued, rehabilitating the concept of the self-sufficient subject?

Interestingly, and perhaps contrary to what might have been expected (the 1980s were undeniably a time of recantations and conversions, religious or otherwise, a time when it was fashionable to take one's distance from the struggles of the Sixties, as well as the discussions that accompanied them), there is very little renunciation of political and theoretical positions in *The Future*. Those who eagerly anticipated a repudiation of Marxism by one of its leading intellectual champions were sorely disappointed, a fact that explains some of the more vicious reviews of *The Future Lasts Forever* (bearing titles like "Marx and Murder" and "The Paris Strangler"), especially in the English-language media. While he is quite critical of the French Communist Party (the PCF), Althusser never conflates the PCF as an institution with Marxism itself (in fact, he accuses the party of suffering from a "fear of the masses" that prevented it from waging a revolutionary struggle in May 1968 – hardly the kind of criticism that British and American conservative critics were hoping to hear) (Althusser 1992, 230). His final word on Marxism is quite striking: he tells us that

> at a time when Marxism is declared dead and buried . . . on the grounds of an unbelievable theoretical eclecticism and poverty, on the pretext of a so-called postmodernity, or, yet again, on the notion that matter has disappeared, having given way to the immaterialities of communication . . . I remain profoundly attached not, of course, to the letter – to which I have never adhered – but to the materialist inspiration of Marx. I am an optimist: I believe that this inspiration will cross every desert and even if it takes new forms – which is inevitable in a world so rapidly changing – it will live again. (Ibid., 223, translation modified)

More specifically, Althusser still holds (*dur comme fer*, "as hard as iron") the same views of philosophy and philosophical practice. His definition of philosophy as "the class struggle in philosophy" (in the last instance), requiring an intervention in a concrete conjuncture in order to change its balance of forces retains for him all its validity and relevance. In keeping with this generalized affirmation of his life's work, even as he reveals its sordid, petty and sometimes disturbing origins in the conflictual history of his own singular psyche, there appears no renunciation of his theoretical anti-humanism, or of the works in which Althusser's critique of the notion of the human being as subject takes shape.

None of this excludes, however, the possibility that without stating a return to humanism and a rehabilitation of the human being as subject, Althusser nevertheless carries it out. After all, as we have already noted, the "golden rule of materialism, 'never judge a man by what he thinks about himself,'" would appear to exclude in advance the project of autobiography, depriving it of both explanatory value and interest. It is precisely this glaring contradiction, symptomatically unacknowledged, that makes *The Future Lasts Forever* what it is. The text finally illustrates what it does not theorize and what Althusser could not completely theorize in his philosophical work. It was Althusser's former student Michel Pêcheux, himself no stranger to madness and tragedy,[1] who used the phrase "the plague of subjection" (*la peste de l'assujettissement*). The process by which Beckett's Molloy, penniless, homeless and crippled, is declared to be free, to be the equal of all others, to be master of his own fate and destiny may be laughably false from the perspective of Spinoza, Marx and Nietzsche, but these ideas are not thereby illusions to be dispelled by the light of knowledge. On the contrary, Althusser strictly maintained that ideology possesses a material existence: the declaration by which we are endowed with the rights (and, yes, the responsibilities) of free sovereign human individuals, that is to say, the ideological interpellation of the individual as subject is not merely a discursive event, a matter of language or even ideology conceived as a set of ideas and myths. Like the plague, it is a matter of bodies and as such cannot be refused by an act of will: the pathologist who perfectly understands its etiology and characteristics is no more immune to the plague than anyone else. Althusser, caught in the web of the ISAs, "assumes the position" of subject, even as that position was denied to him in law by reason of his insanity. He is still the subject of his discourse, the author of a statement, a confession called *The Future Lasts Forever* which, although legally null and void, will nevertheless produce real effects. Accordingly, Althusser reconstructs the sequence of internal causes invisible to the rest of the world, which sees only the effects, a sequence that leads from the moment of his birth ("I was born at 4:30 a.m. on October 16, 1918") to "that Sunday, November 16" in 1980 when he took the life of Hélène Legotien.

In fact, when we turn to Althusser's text, this "critical confession" that is "almost without precedent" (ibid., 29, translation modified), as he describes it, we find that it exhibits all the unacknowledged contradictions, discrepancies and gaps that we have seen in the literary texts previously examined. To confront the work in its literal existence, to read it in the Althusserian manner, that is, to the letter, is to see very clearly the way in which Althusser has eluded himself.

Such a confrontation allows us to assign a certain symptomatic significance to Althusser's "admission" that he only knew a little Hegel by mid-career, a statement that is difficult to reconcile (and he nowhere addresses this inconsistency in his "testimony") with the fact that he had already written a book-length thesis on Hegel which, however we may judge it as a contribution to Hegel scholarship, demonstrates an extremely comprehensive and detailed knowledge of Hegel's texts. In a very importance sense, Althusser's autobiography exhibits the drama and indeed tragedy of consciousness as Hegel describes it in *The Phenomenology of Spirit,* a work that Althusser once described as "beautiful as the night" (Althusser 1969, 220). For Hegel, Consciousness, until it realizes that its separation from nature and thus its specific existence as consciousness is nothing more than a moment in the alienation and self-deception of something greater than itself, into which it will disappear, is condemned to a dilemma that might well be described as tragic. It begins its search for truth by seeking outside of itself the world as it is, independently of the act of knowing – the world in its independent objectivity. No matter how consciousness attempts to subtract itself from what it perceives in order to apprehend that which is, in its purity, it finds that it cannot escape itself. When it then realizes that it must first know itself in order to separate what it brings to the encounter with the Other from the Other itself, and takes itself for its own object, it discovers in the place where the self should be both the presence of an irreducibly foreign Other in its very midst and the absence of the part of itself that it now realizes is contained by the Other outside of and opposed to it.

What, then, is the drama of *The Future Lasts Forever* if not that of Althusser seeking the truth within him only to find an absence, the silence of the tomb not *on* him, imposed from the outside, as he insists, but in him, a dead self-as-other-than-self buried within, whose blank gaze haunts him like an admonition from another world, a world he can never know? And when he turns to the others whose internal world he attempts to fathom, what does Althusser find but the unrecognized parts of himself, both good and bad, that have eluded his searching gaze? We are thus compelled to regard Althusser's attempt to say what he did, what he thought and what he was as an utter failure that reveals rather that Althusser remained finally unintelligible to himself, a riddle masquerading as its own answer, a failure which in turn provides a stunning confirmation of his most important theoretical arguments.

As I noted earlier, the autobiography begins with a minute description of the crime for which he was never indicted, the "statement" to the police and to the court that he was never called upon to give: "what follows, down to the last detail, is my precise memory of those events, forever engraved on my mind . . . the scene of the murder just as I experienced it" (Althusser 1992, 15). At the point the description begins, Legotien is already dead and Althusser "suddenly" becomes aware of himself "kneeling beside her . . . massaging her neck" (ibid., 15). He is able to recall even the minute features of the scene: "The grey light of a November morning – it was almost nine o'clock on Sunday the sixteenth – filtered through the tall window to the left, on to the end of the bed. The window was framed by a pair of very old Empire red curtains which hung there a long time, tattered with age and burnt by the sun." Again, "suddenly" (he repeats the word), he "was terror-struck" as he realized from the expression on her face and the position of her body that she was dead (ibid., 15). He then screamed "I've strangled Hélène," rushing out of his apartment and to the lodgings of the École's physician, Dr. Étienne. The latter returned with Althusser to the scene to determine if Hélène could be revived, only to discover that it was indeed too late.

What is striking, of course, is that the scene Althusser describes is not that of the murder, but its aftermath. Although he is massaging her neck, and not the nape of the neck as usual, but the front, she is already dead. We are thus at the final link in a chain of causes that is otherwise invisible to us. Not only is the account of the murder itself missing, but the events that led to it, the words and actions preceding her death are lacking as well. The "precise memory engraved on" his mind is incomplete and marked by the elision of what alone will make it meaningful, the motives, the intentions, the proximate causes of the act. These are buried in a "zone of darkness," perhaps Althusser's own "inner darkness of exclusion." Later, towards the end of the narrative, Althusser suggests that his analyst had sent an urgent letter to him, strongly recommending that he be hospitalized for acute depression, which for some reason did not reach the École until it was too late. Neither this nor the vague descriptions of their deteriorating relationship even remotely explains why Althusser would strangle his wife. Again, he refers to the "unfathomable night" in which the necessary facts remain lost, the tomb in which they lie buried never to be resuscitated or even exhumed.

In the most important sense, Althusser's text illustrates the dilemma of consciousness that he so well described in his essay on Bertolazzi and Brecht: a "consciousness impatient for truth," unable finally to grasp itself and the reality around it. The movement of the narrative is a movement of perpetual deferral, a movement towards a truth, its own truth, that is always beyond, the always absent center (of initiatives, of thought, speech and action) that exists in the form of a gap in the text which no memory or explanation can fill. We might recall Althusser's fascination with Cremonini's "exploration of mirrors, above all, of the old mirrors found in run-down entry ways, in sordid armoires, circa 1900," places not unlike Althusser's own shabby apartment (ibid., 597). The mirrors adorn what is usually the only piece of furniture in worn, cramped flats: to Althusser, they represented the sole property owned by their proletarian tenants: not the armoire or the mirror itself, of course (the apartments came "furnished"), but the image, their image, reflected in the mirror. But Althusser has missed something crucial about Cremonini's mirrors: they often reflect to the spectator what the figure in the painting does not or cannot see, what is invisible to them, but visible to us. Cremonini paints, then, the inability of his subjects to see themselves; what is essential is not simply *what* they don't see but *that* they don't see. They are defined by the impossibility of seeing themselves, by the lack or absence that greets them when they turn to look at themselves.

The concluding chapter of *The Future Lasts Forever* is particularly revealing in this regard:

> I showed this text to an old doctor friend of mine who had known Hélène and me for a very long time and naturally I put to him the following question:
>
> "What did take place between Hélène and me on that Sunday, November 16th, which resulted in such an appalling murder?"

The entire text that follows, with the exception of two brief concluding sentences, consists of the friend's reply, "word for word." Although the citation is uninterrupted, quotation marks adorn each paragraph as if constantly to remind the reader that this is not Althusser speaking, but another, a doctor and therefore someone who knows more than he knows, even about that fateful Sunday – that scene of which Althusser is simultaneously the sole survivor and the person least capable of understanding. The cited passage refers to Althusser in the second person ("you," "*tu*," the familiar form in

French), as if his truth must be addressed to him by another who sees in him what he cannot see; as if what is most intimate is not contained within him to be recovered, but instead alienated in an Other from whom Althusser must receive his truth. But, of course, the truth even eludes the Other who is supposed to know precisely what Althusser doesn't know and can't know. The doctor friend simply multiplies the hypotheses and questions. His conclusion: "in order to understand the incomprehensible, you have to take into account uncertain and imponderable factors [*des impondérables aléatoires*] (of which there were so many in your case) but also the ambivalent nature of phantasies, which introduces a whole host of opposing possibilities" (ibid., 285). In relation to himself, he has fallen into a most improbable skepticism, a skepticism of the aleatory (a skepticism he elsewhere denounces[2] – a fact that should forestall any psycho-biographical reading of his use of the aleatory in his last phase) which renders him not only unknown but unknowable whether to himself or to the Other. Once again, the truth is deferred in a dialectic that never permits a reconciliation of Althusser with himself, but, like the *dialectique à la cantonnade* that he describes in Bertolazzi and Brecht, continually decenters him, separating him from the truth about him that not even the Other can give to him.

The narrative concludes by looking beyond the Other, to the Other of the Other, to the beyond of the beyond in an infinite play of mirrors that permits no conclusions. His "final word," the last two sentences of *The Future Lasts Forever*, are spoken into the void, into that dark night that is unfathomable because there is nothing in it to be fathomed: "I hope those who think they know more or have more to say will not be afraid to do so. They can only help me live" (ibid., 286).

It is surely significant though that Althusser's text provoked less explanation than judgment (whether idealization or devaluation). This is probably less the effect of Althusser's powers of seduction or, on the contrary, of his self-destructive urges than of the "interference" of his other, previous texts, that is, the effect of Althusser as author. It is difficult to say whether *The Future Lasts Forever* can accurately be classified with Althusser's other works in a unified *oeuvre* according to any other logic than that of property. Does the fact that the author retains the same name and legal identity make him the unifying principle of some very diverse works? In the *Ethics*, Spinoza spoke of a Spanish poet who had undergone such a great transformation in his life that he no longer recalled writing the works of which he was the author and could no longer understand them. Was he in fact the same man who wrote them or would it not be more accurate to describe that man as dead? Spinoza could not decide. Perhaps we can pay no greater homage to Althusser than to regard his *oeuvre* not as an organic whole, unified by his authorial psychology, but as a diverse series of texts, each itself forced apart by the very power imparted to it, the whole nothing more than a still-motion photograph of innumerable splinters of shattered glass as they descend in divergent arcs, never to reach the ground.

Notes

1. Michel Pêcheux, a philosopher who was part of Althusser's circle as a student at the École and who remained close to Althusser theoretically and politically until around 1980, is referred to by name a number of times in the text. He is also cited, without being identified, by Althusser as the protagonist in what he calls "the most touching" encounter during his hospitalization following the murder:

   > An old student who had become a very dear friend and who was an extraordinary man, came to see me. He asked me not to say anything but to listen to him. For two hours he talked not only of himself, of his terrible childhood, of his father who had been in and out of psychiatric hospitals, and finished by telling me: I came to explain why I can't come to see you. I can't cope with it. A year later, when he was undergoing analysis, he planned his suicide over a long period and never confided in anyone, not even the courageous young woman with whom he lived and worked. He threw himself into the Marne, having cut his wrists and weighted himself down with heavy stones. (Althusser, *The Future Lasts Forever* (1992), p. 261).

2. In *Reading Capital,* Althusser argues that "contingency" is another word for what is not known (111).

Conclusion

To conclude our study as Althusser did his own life's work with his autobiography is to risk confusing the reader. Even if we follow Althusser in holding that there exists no intention but that which is incarnate in the work, we cannot help but regard *The Future Lasts Forever* as an extremely ambivalent work that actively both validates and undermines Althusser's accomplishments as a philosopher. The reader's confusion then is objectively determined; once understood as such and no longer regarded as a subjective, personal failure to perform the act of reading competently, the confusion becomes useful, an indicator of powerful and unmastered conflicts within Althusser's works. These conflicts, of course, are not the personal or private dramas that consumed Althusser's life (although they are not completely independent of them either), but are the necessary and constitutive contradictions that accompany theoretical practice as such. To conclude with *The Future Lasts Forever* and to experience the disorientation that it necessarily engenders, is not simply to understand but to feel the irreducible divergence in Althusser's *oeuvre* as a whole. Perhaps this is the meaning of Brecht's theater for Althusser: his theory of philosophy as an intervention in a specific conjunctive to produce certain effects itself calls for theatrical measures. Truth alone is the necessary but insufficient condition of its own dissemination; unarmed prophets come to ruin. Thus it is not only what Althusser says, but the way that conflicting tendencies of thought coexist without the conflict being addressed or even acknowledged, that constitutes the dramatic experience of reading Althusser. The value of the autobiography, that most un- if not anti-Althusserian work, is that, to cite his own words about art, it "makes us feel" the structure of divergence that governs his work, a structure that is not a structure at all but nothing more than the fragile equilibrium of contending forces that makes Althusser's philosophical project what it is.

To characterize the constitutive contradiction of Althusser's work, we might recall Balibar's phrase cited in the Introduction. Although Balibar refers here explicitly to Althusser's treatment of the materialist dialectic in *For Marx,* his comments illuminate a previously unrecognized conflict even in the heart of Althusser's most closely argued works:

> there will thus be Althusserians of the Conjuncture and Althusserians of the Structure (it is still the case today, even if some have changed sides). Perhaps, it is this tension, unresolved, imperceptible and thus kept in the shadows, that permits an extension of the idea of the materialist dialectic.

If we can generalize this formula beyond the context of *For Marx* we might begin not only to specify the divergence that emerges in Althusser's work, but to appreciate its theoretical fecundity.

Interestingly, the first Althusser, according to Balibar, the Althusser of the Conjuncture, is often regarded as the later Althusser (Negri), the Althusser who stresses a materialism of the encounter. It was only in reaction to this initial strain in his thought that he moved toward what Balibar argues is a structuralist conception of history, as if Althusser simultaneously seeks to deny and undo the element that he would belatedly term "aleatory." To take Balibar's suggestions seriously then is to regard the conflict of tendencies within the heart of Althusser's endeavor as definitive, even as a dialectical motor of contradiction driving his thought forward without any possibility of a final resolution. Indeed, how might we reconcile the demand for a science of history (in which the study of literature, art and culture would have a place) with the emphasis on the singular and the unpredictable, the critique of all forms of irrationalism and skepticism with the notion of the imponderably aleatory. Finally, we cannot help but acknowledge that the critic of every philosophy of the origin in fact posited an original chaos or primal disorder beneath the appearance of order.

The existence of this unresolved tension in Althusser undoubtedly helps to explain the fact that his work continues to be read and regarded as relevant in cultural studies (in the broad sense) even today. In fact, Althusser would appear to embody the opposition between postmodernism and modernism, between rationalism and irrationalism, and can be summoned in defense of either of the opposing sides. Before we begin to speak of the postmodem

Althusser, however, we would do well to consider the ways in which his thought is irreducible to these distinctions. For, if Althusser rejected any notion of a logic of scientific discovery or *a priori* method that would serve to guarantee the truth of a given scientific practice and its findings, he never did so on the basis of another opposing *a priori* postulate, i.e., that there can be no truth, no science, or that art exceeds our capacity to speak of or know it. On the contrary, he rejected these alternatives of transcendental reason (high postmodernism is transcendentalism in an almost pure form) in favor of the primacy of scientific practice over theory, speaking of the necessity of writing a history of the sciences as it was, with its accidents and chance encounters, its regressions as well as its advances, and not as this history should have been according to some model of linear progression.

What does this mean to the student of literature and culture? Among other things, it serves to remind us that the object of our work is not to appreciate or consume (or help others appreciate or consume) the objects we analyze but to produce knowledge. In turn, we produce knowledge by recognizing the historical conditions that determine how and what we know (to paraphrase Spinoza, there is always knowledge), and conversely what specific obstacles prevent us from knowing more. Althusser and Macherey have identified many of the theoretical obstacles that block the way of knowledge in the realm of culture. All are bound by a common objective: to deny the objective reality or materiality of the works and practices that constitute culture. As we have seen, even the attempt to explain culture historically can take the form of a reduction of cultural artifacts to something more real. The call to understand art always in relation to a specific historical context, as we have noted, produces more questions than answers, as well as a few answers to questions that have yet to be posed.

We may conclude by stating a few propositions derived from our reading of Althusser; these propositions should be regarded as provisional, meaning that even as they help us think about culture, the results of our thinking may and almost certainly will lead us to return to and revise these propositions in certain ways:

1. The work of art is irreducible, it must be explained as it is. To explain the work as it is, is to surrender any notion of formal perfection, coherence or harmony, together with any notion that

works of art can be understood as systems of elements. It is to cease to search for the originating principle to which it would be reduced by the act of knowledge, the individual intention of a single author or the collective intention of a historical epoch. Paradoxically, only when we reject the notion of author as origin, can we begin to study the historically specific ways in which individuals are "recruited" and interpellated as authors by different ideological and repressive apparatuses.

2. Once we recognize the irreducible materiality of works, the conflicts and contradictions proper to them become visible and knowable. It is here, inside the work, that history appears, the history that is itself a conflict of forces without origin, end or internal rationality. This is another way of saying that the work has neither inside nor outside, no surface or depth (or, if such notions are in some way inescapable, we might say that the work is all surface without depth, everything is displayed and nothing hidden) and that it is in no way external to history or "reality".
3. The knowledge of a given cultural artifact is not limited to the historical conditions of its emergence. It can never be explained once and for all. The work is incomplete and unfinishable. The border that divides it from other works is permeable and constantly fluctuating; it encounters other works, those contemporaneous with it and those from other times, and such encounters bring about a reordering or even a rewriting of the works, imposing new meanings and making visible in them what was previously invisible. The fact that literary works are in some sense never completed no more inhibits the development of a rigorous knowledge than does the fact, in the case of biology, that evolution continues.

It is possible that by working on these propositions derived from Althusser and his circle and by putting them to work in the field of culture, that we will contribute not only to a knowledge of the social world, but to its transformation, which is, after all, that to which Althusser devoted his life.

Appendix: Louis Althusser, "On Brecht and Marx"

I am embarrassed to address the Piccolo Teatro and its friends because I am ignorant in all questions concerning theater. I can claim some little knowledge in philosophy and politics, I know a little bit about Marx and Lenin – that's all.

As for the theater, all I can say is that I very much like the productions of the Piccolo Teatro. Unfortunately I have seen only *El Nost Milan*,[1] the *Baruffe Chiozzotte*, and the *Arlecchino*. However, these three plays made a strong impression on me. *El Nost Milan* has played an important role in my philosophical research. In seeing *El Nost Milan* I understood a little better certain important points in Marx's thought.

I will add that I also know the theoretical writings of Brecht on theater. I read them recently.[2] They are completely astounding for a Marxist philosopher.

You see, my relationship with the theater has mainly a philosophical and political character. Of course, I have also the direct relationship of a spectator with the plays I have seen. Yet, my experience is much too limited. You have to know this in order to correct what I can tell you. Basically, I am speaking about theater *from outside*, as a philosopher and political person (*politique*), as a Marxist philosopher. I am asking you, therefore, to show great severity and at the same time make some allowances.

If, being only a philosopher, I dare to speak about theater, it is because it seems to me that Brecht, who knew the theater, gives me the right to do so. Indeed, Brecht never tired, throughout his life, of directly relating theater to philosophy.

A political theater

In 1929, he wrote: "The theater's future is philosophical" ("Last Stage: *Oedipus*").[3] In 1953, i.e., twenty-four years later, he took up the same thesis again, giving it all its strength ("Notes on Erwin Strittmatter's Play Katzgraben").[4] He then wrote:

> My theater . . . is in the naïve sense of this concept a philosophical theater; that is to say, I am concerned with people's actions and opinions (*Verhalten und Meinen*) . . . I might perhaps, in my defense, point to the case of Einstein, who told the physicist Infeld that ever since childhood, he had merely reflected on the man running after a ray of light and the man shut in a falling elevator. And think what complications that led to! The principle I would like to apply in the theater is that one should not be satisfied with an interpretation of the world; one also has to change it. The changes, great or small, that resulted from this intention – and of which I myself only slowly became aware – were always changes within the framework of the theater, which means that a great number of ancient rules have naturally remained unaltered. It is in this little "naturally" that lies my fault. I hardly ever got round to mentioning these unchanged ancient rules and a number of those who read my hints and explanations imagined that I wanted to suppress them as well. The critics should first go see, as simple spectators, my theater, instead of immediately focusing on my theories, and they will see simply theater, a theater, I hope, full of fantasy, humor, and ideas. Only when they begin to analyze its effects will they be struck by some novelty, of which they could subsequently find the explanation in my theoretical remarks.[5]

Allow me to sum up, in the way of a dutiful philosopher, the essential points of this key text. Brecht states, directly or indirectly, a certain number of precise Theses. I will go back and explain them very schematically. Here is what Brecht tells us:

1. The theater exists. It is a historical and cultural fact; it is a fact.
2. I did not want to suppress these ancient rules. That is to say: I did not want to suppress the *theater*. Because it is precisely the respect of these ancient rules that makes the theater *theater*. This thesis is extremely important. It means that the theater is not life, that the theater is not science, that the theater is not propaganda or direct political agitation. This does not mean that Brecht neglects the

importance of life, of science, and of politics: on the contrary, he thinks that these realities are essential for the theater, and nobody has said it as forcefully as Brecht. But it means that, for him, the theater should remain theater, that is to say, art. This is clear in his invitation: go to see my plays; you will see "simply theater, and I hope, a theater full of fantasy, humour, and ideas."

3. I have only introduced some changes inside the theater, inside the "playing" of the theater, in order to produce certain new effects.[6] "Playing" should be understood in its double sense. First, in the traditional sense of theatrical playing (the theater is playing: the [*actors*] play; the theater is a fictive representation of reality. Playing is not life; it is not reality. What is represented on the stage is not life in person, science in person, politics in person. It is represented, hence it is not *present*). But "playing" should be understood in the second sense: theater allows this "playing" (in the sense that there is some "play" in a door, a hinge, a mechanism). This means that it belongs to the nature of the theater to contain *some room*, some "play" where these changes can be introduced.
4. The changes I have introduced in the theater depend on my philosophical will. This philosophy is summed up by Marx's phrase in the famous 11th Thesis on Feuerbach: the philosophers have been satisfied with interpreting the world; the point is to change it. The philosophy that led Brecht to the changes he has introduced in the "playing" of the theater is Marxist philosophy.

This is precisely what seems to me striking: a parallel between Brecht's revolution in the theater and Marx's revolution in philosophy. Brecht was not a philosopher, one would say, and the philosophy professors are not going to look for lessons about philosophy in Brecht. Why? Because he has not written any philosophical book, has not produced any philosophical system, did not undertake any theoretical discourse in philosophy. Brecht himself used to say that he was philosophically naïve. The philosophy professors are wrong. Brecht has well understood what was essential in Marx's philosophical revolution. He has understood it *practically,* not in a theoretical discourse but in what I would call his *theatrical practice.* Brecht never talks about theatrical practice but always about changes in theatrical *technique.* Thus he seems to talk only about technique. But there is no naked technique: a technique is always inserted into a practice, it is always the technique of *a certain* practice. Brecht's technical revolutions in the theater should be understood as the effects of a revolution in theatrical *practice*.[7] This is very clear in Brecht's texts: his reforms of theatrical technique always depend on an overall conception of the *mise en scène*, which itself depends on a certain conception of the subject, which depends on a certain relation of stage to public, of actors to public, which depends on a certain conception of the relation of theater to history, which depends on a certain philosophical conception. All these terms force one to consider Brecht's technical reforms as the effects of a revolution in theatrical practice.

Here is the essential point: Marx's philosophical revolution is in every respect similar to Brecht's theatrical revolution – it is a revolution in philosophical *practice*.

Brecht does not suppress the theater. The theater exists; it plays a determinate role. Marx does not suppress philosophy. Philosophy exists; it plays a determinate role. Brecht does not create from scratch a new theater, or an anti-theater, or a theater that would break with all past theater, that would, e.g., suppress the entire repertory. Marx and Marxists, as well, do not create from scratch a new philosophy, an anti-philosophy, or a philosophy that would break with all past philosophical tradition. Brecht takes the theater as it exists and acts within the theater such as it exists. Marx, as well, takes philosophy as it exists and acts within philosophy such as it exists. What Brecht revolutionizes is the way of practicing theater: the novelty he brings about is a new *practice* of the theater. In the same way, what Marx revolutionizes in philosophy is the way of practicing philosophy: the novelty he brings about is a new practice of philosophy, not – pace Gramsci – a new philosophy, a philosophy of praxis, but a new practice of philosophy.[8] One can say in exactly the same way: Brecht's theater is not the theater of praxis; its novelty consists in a new theatrical practice.

We should go much further. What allows Marx and Brecht to propose a new practice in philosophy and in the theater? A basic condition: the *knowledge* of the nature and mechanisms of philosophy (for Marx) and of the theater (for Brecht).

This is a determining point. It does not matter if this knowledge of the nature and mechanisms of philosophy and of the theater is contained or not in great theoretical books. It is desirable but not absolutely necessary. Today we still do not have an adequate theory of the nature and mechanisms either of philosophy or of the theater. From this point of view, Marx and Lenin are as "naïve" vis-à-vis the theory of the nature and mechanisms of philosophy as Brecht is naïve vis-à-vis the nature and mechanisms of the theater. They are, as it were, theoretically naïve, from the point of view of philosophy professors, who always need explicit and perfect theoretical treatises. For us, however, what count are new facts, new practices, even if these facts and these revolutionary practices are not presented in explicit and perfect theoretical discourses. It is in the philosophical practice of Marx and Lenin, and in the theatrical practice of Brecht, that we can discover their, more or less explicit, knowledge of the nature and mechanisms of their object: philosophy and the theater.

If we examine these two practices, we can register this common result: it is obvious that Marx and Lenin in philosophy and Brecht in the theater know perfectly well, they have understood, that both philosophy and the theater are deeply involved with the sciences on the one hand, and with politics on the other. This is the first point.

Smothering the voice of politics

This fact is not sufficient, however. In order to simplify the matter, I put aside the relation with the sciences and focus on the relation with politics. Marx and Brecht have understood, each in his own way, that the distinctive feature of philosophy and of the theater was to enter into a mystified relationship with politics. Philosophy and the theater are profoundly determined by politics and yet they do everything in order to efface this determination, to negate it, to appear as if they escaped politics. At the heart of philosophy as well as at the heart of the theater, it is always politics that speaks. But when philosophy and the theater speak, they end up by muffling the voice of politics. Philosophy and the theater always speak in order to cover the voice of politics; and they succeed very well. One can even say that, in the great majority of cases, the function of philosophy and of the theater consists in smothering the voice of politics. They exist only through politics and, at the same time, they exist in order to suppress politics, to which they owe their existence. The result is well known: philosophy keeps denying its involvement in politics, pretends to be above the political class struggle, to address all human beings, to speak in the name of Humanity, without taking sides, i.e., without naming the political party it sides with. This is what Marx calls the philosophy that is satisfied with interpreting the world. In fact no philosophy is satisfied with interpreting the world: all philosophy is politically active, but most philosophies keep denying this activity. They say: we do not take sides, we are satisfied with interpreting the world, with saying what it is. This is what Freud calls a *denegation*. When somebody tells you: I am not involved in politics, you can be certain that in fact he is. The same is true of the theater. Brecht gave the right name to this theater that is involved in politics but maintains that it is not: the theater of an evening's entertainment, culinary theater, the theater of simple aesthetic enjoyment (*jouissance*). Thus, there is a shameful philosophy as there is a shameful theater. Shameful philosophy is sick of speculation. Shameful theater is sick of aestheticism, sick of stageworthiness (theatricality). In both cases we note the appearance of an actual religion, a fascination, a vertigo, a hypnosis, a pure enjoyment. Philosophy becomes an object of consumption and of speculative enjoyment, the theater becomes an object of consumption and of aesthetic enjoyment. Philosophers end up by producing philosophies for consumption and speculative enjoyment; playwrights, directors, and actors end up by producing plays for consumption and aesthetic, culinary, etc. enjoyment. The critique of speculation–interpretation of the world in Marx, and the critique of culinary theater and opera in Brecht, are one and the same critique.

Hence the revolution of the *practice* in Marx and in Brecht. It is not a question of producing a new philosophy, or a new theater. It is a question of establishing a new practice inside philosophy in order to prevent it from being an interpretation of the world, that is, a mystification, and to let it contribute to the transformation of the world; it is a question of establishing a new practice in the theater in order to prevent it from being a mystification, that is, a culinary entertainment, and to let it contribute to the transformation of the world as well. The first effect of the new practice should thus concern the destruction of the mystification of philosophy and of the theater: not suppressing philosophy and the theater but suppressing their mystification. Thus, it is a question of being blunt (*appeler les choses par leur nom*), of taking philosophy and the theater for what they really are (*les appeler par leur nom*), of putting them in their (true) place, of making one see this mystification as a mystification, and, at the same time, of showing the real function of philosophy and of the theater. All this must be done, of course, in philosophy and in the theater. In order to put philosophy and the theater in their (true) place, one has to carry out a *displacement* (*spostamento*) within philosophy and within the theater.[9]

The party position

Here, as well, things are similar in Marx and Brecht. It is in this sense that Brecht's *Verfremdungseffekt* should be understood; to the standard (and not incorrect) French translation, *effet de distanciation* ("distancing effect"), I would still prefer *effet de déplacement* ("displacement effect") or *effet de décalage* ("shifting effect").

This effect should not be understood only as an effect of the theatrical techniques but as a general effect of the revolution in theatrical practice. It is not a question of changing the place of some small elements in the play of the actors, it is a question of a displacement that affects the whole of the theater's conditions. The same rule holds for philosophy. It is thus a question of the **totality of displacements** that constitute this new practice.

Among all these displacements there is a fundamental displacement, which is the cause of all the others and, at the same time, sums them up: the *displacement of the point of view.* The great lesson of Marx and Brecht is that one should displace the general point of view from which all questions of philosophy and of the theater are considered. One has to abandon the point of view of the speculative interpretation of the world (philosophy) or of culinary aesthetic enjoyment (theater), and move to occupy another place, which is, roughly speaking, that of *politics.* I said that in philosophy and in the theater, it is politics that speaks, but that its voice is, generally, muffled. One has to yield the floor to politics, and hence displace the voice of philosophy and the voice of the theater in order to hear the words pronounced from the place of politics. This is what Lenin calls the party position in philosophy. There is in Brecht an entire series of expressions that amounts to saying: one has to occupy a party position in the theater. One should not identify the latter with the party position in politics; philosophy and the theater (or art) *are not politics.* Philosophy is something other than science and something other than politics. The theater is something other than science and politics. Thus, we must not identify philosophy and science, philosophy and politics, theater and science, theater and politics. We must occupy in philosophy as well as in the theater the place that *represents politics.* Of course, in order to occupy it we must find it, and this is not easy because in order to know the place of politics in philosophy and in the theater, we must know how philosophy and the theater function, and *how* politics (and science) are represented there. One cannot see the place of politics in the theater with a naked eye. (It is probable that this place displaces itself in history, or, to be more precise, it is probable that politics changes its *representatives* in the history of philosophy and of the theater.)

Once we have carried out this fundamental displacement, all other displacements follow. In reality, all this happens simultaneously. I make these distinctions for the sake of clarity. In reality, there is no distinction.

All the effects of displacement mentioned by Brecht are the effects of this fundamental displacement. I shall try to enumerate them.

1. We must first *displace the theater in respect to the ideology of the theater* that exists in the head of the spectators. For that, we must "show" that the theater is theater, only theater, and not life. We must show that the stage is a stage, artificially erected before the spectators, and not a prolongation of the auditorium. We must show that there is between the auditorium and the stage a gap, a distance. We must show this distance *on the stage* itself. Hence, a series of technical reforms concerning set, lights, props, costumes, posters, signs, songs, etc. We must break the complicity between the spectators and the spectacle, which is a mystified complicity. It is the matter of a *physical* displacement, which would show what the theater and the spectators do not want to see, namely, that the theater is not life.
2. We must then *displace the conception of the play* in respect to the traditional conception. This is what Brecht had in mind when he talked about the "*epic style.*" It involves first of all the conception of the director, and, of course, the conception of the playwright when he is writing a play. But the conception of the director is primordial. One can perform a good play badly,[10] and perform an inferior play very well.[11] This displacement essentially consists in decentering the play, in avoiding the form of a spontaneous representation that the audience has of life and its conflicts, of the drama and its solution. Schematically and symbolically, one can say that the play should not have its center in itself but outside, or that there should be no hero in the play, any more than a great scene where everything is present and summed up – a great scene of classical conflict. Brecht's stroke of genius, for example, consisted in not showing the great scene of the trial in his play *Galileo* (cf. Dort[12]). Everybody expects to see the trial of Galileo. Everybody expects to

hear Galileo pronounce the historical phrase about the earth: "*eppur si muove*!" ("yet, it turns!"). Brecht does not show the trial and Galileo does not utter the historical phrase. The result is that the center of the play is not within the play but outside, and one does not see it, ever.

3. We must, finally, *displace the play of the actors* in respect to the idea of acting that the spectators and the actors themselves have. The great technical innovations of Brecht in this domain are well known. It is in relation to himself that the actor has to keep a "distance": the actor has to displace himself in relation to the ideology of the actor. Ordinarily, these innovations of Brecht are seen as purely technical. To be sure, Brecht has modified the technique of acting, but this technique belongs to a much wider modification, that of theatrical practice in its entirety. Separated from the rest, it functions in a vacuum. Today everybody applies Brecht's techniques. One can safely affirm that the reduction of Brecht's revolution in theatrical practice to simple [. . .] technical recipes constitutes a betrayal of Brecht's revolution. A practice is an altogether different thing from a technique.

The end of identification

The result of all these displacements produces a new relation between spectacle and audience. It is a *displaced* relation. Brecht has expressed this effect of displacement as the V-effect,[13] in the audience itself, as the end of *identification*. The spectators should cease to identify with what the stage shows, should occupy a critical position, and take sides, judge, vote, make up their mind, decide. A play does not decide for them. A play is not ready-made clothing. A play is not clothing. The audience should tailor their own clothing in the fabric of a play, or rather in the pieces of fabric given by a play. For there is no ready-made clothing in the play. In simple terms, there is no hero.

I do not have enough time to show that exactly the same method of displacement is at work in Marx's philosophical revolution. The latter consists in provoking displacements in philosophy that have a double objective: to suppress practically the effects of philosophical mystification and to allow those who are touched by Marxist philosophical practice to make up their mind with full knowledge of the facts.

There remains, however, an important difference: in spite of all resemblances, *the theater is not philosophy*: the matter of the theater is not the matter of philosophy. The theater is art and philosophy is theory.

It is perhaps here that Brecht reaches his limits. To be sure, he says correctly that the theater should show politics and science but remain theater, for the theater is something specific. He does not say very clearly, however, in what this specificity consists; he does not name the specific difference that makes the theater theater, and not another thing. Yet, Brecht does give us certain positive indications. For example, he says that the theater should *show* something, make us see, in a concrete, visible manner, in actors' behavior; this is the peculiar characteristic of the theater. He also says that the theater should *entertain*. The peculiar characteristic of the theater is to show something important in an entertaining way. How is it possible to show and to entertain at the same time, and whence comes entertainment? Brecht's explications here are not entirely adequate. He tends to identify "showing" and making knowledge (science). (There is a bit of the *Aufklärer* or Enlightener in Brecht: the theme of "theater of the scientific era," etc.) He tends to interpret entertainment as a joy, joy of understanding, joy of feeling oneself capable of taking part in the transformation of the world – joy of transformation. He tends to bring into a direct relation, by short-circuiting, the transformation of the world with the transformation of the spectator, the science of the modern age with the objective knowledge that the theater imparts to the spectator. However, these explanations run into difficulties. Brecht himself pointed to the essential difficulty when he said that what happens on the [*stage of*] the theater is neither science nor life, and that one has to disconcert the spectator, to thwart his expectations. How can this deception be at the same time a joy? And what relationship is there between this joy and the entertainment that the theater should necessarily provide? Brecht's theoretical explanations are inadequate but, once again, one should not believe that all Brecht is in his theoretical explanations. There is much more in his practice than in his theoretical explanations. For my part, I would like to draw some supplementary theoretical explanations from Brecht's practice, and also from that of Strehler.

Theater and the risk of fire

First, I shall ask a simple question, answered by Brecht himself: what is the *matter* of theatrical representation, what are the components of the *matter* that allow the theatrical representation to take place, both from the side of the public and of the actors? This is a fact: the theater exists. But in order that it exist something must happen between the public and the stage; there must be something that allows the theatrical communication, on which theatrical practice works. Brecht correctly identifies this object *as opinions and actions of people.* In our Marxist theoretical language, we shall say that the matter of the theater is *ideology* (*l'idéologique*). Ideology does not only mean ideas or systems of ideas but – as Gramsci has seen perfectly well – at once ideas *and* actions, ideas *in* actions, which form a unity. When spectators come to the theater, they have in their heads and their bodies ideas and actions. On the stage they are shown ideas and actions, ideas in actions; they are shown a certain ideology (*de l'idéologique*). It is the fact that the audience comes to see on the stage what they have in their heads and bodies that sanctions the existence of the theater. To cite an old formula, which is not false, what the audience looks for in the theater is itself. The theater is like a mirror where the spectators come to see what they have in their head and body; they come to *recognize* themselves. This is all-important, as we know that the function of ideology is *recognition* (and not knowledge, *cognition*). The evidence can be found in the spontaneous popular reaction before a successful theatrical representation of a character. The audience says: "That's exactly right! How true!" (*C'est bien ça! Comme c'est vrai*). This is the very expression of *recognition,* as before of a portrait: "It is really him." When it comes to the theater the spectators always hope for the justification of the final "c'est bien ça." When they recognize themselves, when they are certain to have recognized themselves, they are content. First satisfaction.

In order to be really delightful, however, the pleasure of the ideological recognition of oneself must contain a certain risk, the risk of a certain danger. When we go to the theater looking for a suitable confirmation of ourselves, a suitable recognition of ourselves, it means that we are not absolutely sure of ourselves, that we doubt ourselves a little. To be sure, we do not admit this doubt; it nevertheless belongs to the pleasure we expect. This is why the theater creates pleasure only by *playing* with this risk, with this danger, with this doubt – in order finally to dismiss all risk, all danger, and all doubt. By playing with fears, with doubts, with risks, the theater says aloud what one thinks only in silence. This gives a double pleasure to the spectator. At first, we laugh because we believe that it is *always others* who fear, who doubt, etc. Then, we are pleased because in the end everything always works out, one way or another, and the pleasure is multiplied by the dangers one has narrowly escaped. At the end, we recognize ourselves and we say: "this is true," which means that we have recognized ourselves and have been justified. When the spectators come to see the play, they accept the rule of the game: precisely that one "plays" with their ideas and their actions, in order to *show* them that their ideas and their actions do not run any risk. Aristotle said that the theater is a catharsis, and Freud that art is a fictive triumph. Let us translate: a fictive triumph means a fictive risk. In the theater the spectators are given the pleasure of seeing fire played with, only to be reassured that there is no fire, or that the fire is not in their house but in somebody else's house, anyway not in theirs.

If we want to know why the theater entertains, we must take into account this particular type of pleasure – playing with fire without danger – with its double stipulation: 1. It is a fire without danger because it is on the stage, and because the play always extinguishes the fire; and 2. When there is a fire, it is always at a neighbor's house.

Here, we must say a word about neighbors, that is, the audience. The audience is, indeed, composed of neighbors. It was pointed out a long time ago that what distinguishes theater from cinema is the spectacle in the auditorium. This is true historically: in the theater one finds and can recognize different classes of society, as a body or represented by more or less numerous delegations. A theater hall with its different seats, good and bad, with its intermissions, with its conversations, is a small society, where social relations and their differences are reproduced. The lower classes come to see the rich and powerful. The latter are aware of being watched. In the theater, people see and look at one another and themselves. They see each other and themselves in a double sense: in the auditorium and then on the stage. The neighbors, in whose house there is a fire on the stage, are also, as if by accident, in the auditorium. The lower classes, who, in the auditorium, watch the rich and powerful with respect, laugh at them when there is a fire in their house on the stage, or they find them magnificent on the stage as well, overcoming the crises of their life and their conscience.[14]

Translated by Max Statkiewicz

Notes

I am grateful to Michael Sprinker for his comments and suggestions [Translator].

1. Cf. Louis Althusser, "Le 'Piccolo', Bertolazzi et Brecht (Notes sur un théâtre matérialiste)," first published in *Esprit* (December 1962), and then in Louis Althusser, *Pour Marx* (Paris: Maspero, 1965), pp. 129–52 [François Matheron]; English translation by Ben Brewster in Louis Althusser, *For Marx* (Harmondsworth, UK: Allen Lane, 1969), pp. 129–51 [Translator].
2. Althusser's typescript notes on Brecht's writings on theater have been preserved in the Althusser Archives [François Matheron].
3. Bertolt Brecht, *Écrit sur le théâtre* (Paris: L'Arche, 1963), p. 24 [François Matheron]; English translation by John Willett, *Brecht on Theatre* (New York: Hill and Wang, 1964), p. 24 [Translator].
4. Bertolt Brecht, *Écrit sur le théâtre,* pp. 265–6 [François Matheron]; Willett, *Brecht on Theatre,* p. 248. The relationship between the epic theater and philosophy is a constant theme in Brecht's writings; see especially "Der Philosoph im Theater" and "Das epische Theater" in *Schriften zum Theater 1,* in *Gesammelte Werke 15* (Frankfurt am Main: Suhrkamp Verlag, 1967), pp. 252ff. and 266 (Willett, *Brecht on Theatre,* pp. 72); the latter contains an earlier reference to Marx's eleventh thesis on Feuerbach [Translator].
5. In my translation of Brecht's text I follow, with a few exceptions, Willet's translation; the exceptions accommodate the particularities of the French translation used by Althusser [Translator].
6. Since in French, a dramatic text is not called *jeu* (play) but *pièce* (*de théâtre*), I translate *jeu* as "playing" rather than "play" [Translator].
7. Uncertain text; the typescript reads: "*La révolution de Brecht dans la technique théâtrale doivent être comprises comme des effects d'une révolution dans la pratique théâtrale*" ("Brecht's revolution in the technique of the theater should be understood as the effects of a revolution in the theatrical practice") preceded by a passage crossed out by Althusser: "*Les révolutions techniques de Brecht doivent être comprises comme . . .*"

("Brecht's technical revolutions should be understood as . . .") [François Matheron].

8. Let us recall that the penultimate paragraph of "Lenin and Philosophy" (a communication presented to the Société Française de Philosophie on February 24, 1968) ends with a practically identical formula: "Marxism is not a (new) philosophy of praxis, but a (new) practice of philosophy" – Louis Althusser, *Lenin and Philosophy and other Essays*, trans. Ben Brewster (London: New Left Books, 1971), p. 68 [François Matheron].
9. The sonorous word *spostamento* belongs to the intended Italian setting of Althusser's talk [Translator].
10. Althusser gives the example of Brecht's *Mother Courage*, staged in the Théâtre National Populaire by Jean Villar in 1951 [François Matheron].
11. It is, of course, Strehler's production of Bertolazzi's *El Nost Milan* that Althusser has in mind – a production that aroused his enthusiasm in July 1962, and marked his theory of ideology; see Althusser, "The 'Piccolo Teatro': Bertolazzi and Brecht (Notes on a Materialist Theatre)," in *For Marx*, pp. 129–51; cf. Étienne Balibar, "The Non-Contemporaneity of Althusser," in E. Ann Kaplan and Michael Sprinker (eds), *The Althusserian Legacy* (London: Verso, 1993), p. 16 [Translator].
12. Probable reference to Bernard Dort, "Galilée et le cocher de fiacre," in Théâtre publique. *Essais de critique* (Paris: Seuil, 1967), pp. 188–96 [François Matheron].
13. See Brecht, "A Short Description of a New Technique of Dramatic Art, which Produces a *Verfremdungseffekt*" and "A Short Organum for the Theatre," in *Gesammelte Werke 15*, 341ff. and *16*, 680ff. [François Matheron]; Willet, *Brecht on Theatre*, 143ff. and 192f., respectively. *Verfremdungseffekt* is most often translated into English as "estrangement effect" or "alienation effect." The latter has been criticized for its possible confusion with the translation of Marxian *Entfremdung*; see e.g., Peter Brooker, "Key words in Brecht's theory and practice," in Peter Thomson and Glendyr Sacks (eds), *The Cambridge Companion to Brecht* (Cambridge: Cambridge University Press, 1994), p. 193, and Fredric Jameson, *Brecht and Method* (London: Verso, 1998), p. 85 note 13. Brecht himself had used the term *Entfremdung* before having definitely settled on *Verfremdung*; see, e.g., *Gesammelte Werke 15*, 265 [Translator].
14. The text stops here, obviously unfinished [François Matheron].

Annotated Bibliography

The major texts by Althusser

For Marx (1969)

Although not Althusser's first book (*Montesquieu* was published in 1959), it nevertheless remains the definitive statement of his re-reading of Marx and Lenin. It is here that he attempts to define what is unprecedented in their thought, what is irreducible to earlier thinkers, such as Hegel and Feuerbach, however great their influence on and authority for Marx and Lenin. In "Contradiction and Overdetermination," Althusser attempts to establish the specificity of the materialist conception of historical contradiction through an examination of Lenin. In opposition to the Hegelian contradiction, which is always binary, the Marxist contradiction is the outcome of a multiplicity of factors, not all of which are rooted in economic developments. Althusser rejects any teleological or functionalist conception of historical change. "On the Materialist Dialectic" develops these themes at greater length as Althusser responds to critics of the earlier essay. Perhaps even more important, however, is his critique of humanism, his extracting from Marx (primarily, but not exclusively, the later Marx) of a theoretical anti-humanism that rejects the notion of the human individual endowed with certain invariant charateristics as an explanatory principle of history. Theoretical anti-humanism, in contrast, poses the question of the historical forms of individualization and even the emergence of the human in history.

Reading Capital (1975)

Althusser's contribution to *Reading Capital* is perhaps second only to *For Marx* in its importance as a key to Althusser's thought. The original French version, published in 1965, has not been translated in its entirety; in addition to the texts by Althusser and Balibar which appear in the English version, there were texts by three other authors: Pierre Macherey, Jacques Rancière, and Roger Establet. It represents the fruits of Althusser's seminar on *Capital*, which took place at the Ecole Normale Supérieure from January to April 1965. Althusser's text is by far his most difficult by virtue of its remarkable density; it is also filled, however, with some of his most precious theoretical insights, many of which have yet to be noted. In addition to his remarkable exploration of what it is to read a theoretical text, his critique of Hegelian and structuralist notions of the social whole, his conception of the history of science as having little to do with a logic of scientific discovery, there are valuable discussions of Husserl's phenomenology and Sartre's notion of historical determination. It is famous or perhaps infamous for proposing the idea of structural causality, an idea which served as proof to Althusser's critics of his structuralist propensities, despite the thoroughgoing critique of structuralism elsewhere in the text. It was later recognized to be an expression of Althusser's Spinozism.

Lenin and Philosophy, and Other Essays (1971)

This collection contains some of Althusser's most influential texts from the period 1966–70. The title essay, "Lenin and Philosophy," marked Althusser's rethinking of philosophy. In a presentation to the Société Française de la Philosophie, he announced that philosophy was no longer "the Theory of theoretical practices" but instead itself a form of theoretical practice. Philosophy exists in the practice of drawing lines of demarcation to make visible the antagonistic elements in a given theoretical field. By the drawing of a line or rather the making visible of a contradiction, philosophy helps differentiate science from the ideology that inevitably accompanies it, hindering its work and attempting to exploit it to the benefit of the established order. In addition to the writings on art and literature discussed previously, the collection contains Althusser's single most influential essay: "Ideology and the Ideological State Apparatuses," which radically recasts the notion of ideology. Instead of false consciousness, mass deception or distorted communication, Althusser argues that ideology possess a material existence in rituals and apparatuses which have the body as their object. The individual subject is then an effect rather than a cause, addressed as the author of actions and speech, the causes of which are beyond, and unknown to, the individual. A new edition appeared in 2002, with a remarkable preface by Fredric Jameson that indicates a new openness to the thought of Althusser.

Politics and History (1972)

This collection contains three very important works by Althusser. The first is the entire text of his first major work, *Montesquieu: Politics and History*, originally published in 1959 – a work that is not only a landmark in the study of this eighteenth-century thinker, but is perhaps the first time Althusser put into practice his method of reading texts by restoring to them the contradictions proper to them. In this case problems engendered by Montesquieu's concept of "spirit," anticipate not only those Hegel would encounter in his concept of totality, but also the problems posed by the idea of social structure so current in the 1950s and 1960s. The text "Rousseau: the Social Contract" is similarly interesting both for its analysis of the concept of social contract and for the careful description of the discrepancies that drive Rousseau's text to the impasse that impelled him out of the philosophical realm and into "the other of theory," literature. Finally, "On Marx's Relation to Hegel" marks the beginning of a reclamation of Hegel after the anti-Hegelian tone of the earlier works, insisting that Hegel's philosophy proposes a conception of history as a process without a subject and therefore marks a break with any philosophy of consciousness.

Essays in Self-Criticism (1973)

Collected here are three important works by Althusser, all from the early to mid-1970s. They represent interesting attempts on Althusser's part to reflect critically upon the work of the previous decade and to confront the actual effects of his work. Two of the three texts were published as separate books in French: *The Reply to John Lewis* and *Elements of Self-Criticism*. In 1972, Althusser composed a response to a very unflattering and occasionally personal attack on him by a member of the Communist Party of Great Britain. In his response to Lewis's rousing defense of Marxist humanism, Althusser takes the opportunity to refine further his definition of philosophy: "philosophy is, in the last instance, class struggle in the field of theory" (72). Philosophical struggles produce real effects; they advance or inhibit the struggle waged by the working class by clarifying or obscuring the reality and stakes of their struggle. *Elements of Self-Criticism* destabilizes certain of the most important formulas in Althusser's 1965 texts, notably the break between the young and the mature Marx and the distinction between science and ideology. Althusser, further, takes the opportunity to explain why he and his students were never structuralists. He insists that what readers mistook for structuralism was in fact Spinozism, which in turn constituted "one of the greatest lessons in heresy the world has ever seen." Finally, apart from a very short contribution to a debate within the French Communist Party, the remainder of the work consists of Althusser's 1975 *Soutenance* or Doctoral defense, "Is it Simple to be a Marxist in Philosophy?" Althusser argues that it is no longer a question of constructing a coherent, self-contained Marxist philosophy, but rather one of learning to intervene in the entire field of philosophy, to disengage the materialist element even in philosophical doctrines that once would have been regarded as purely idealist, such as Scholasticism or Medieval Jewish philosophy, and the idealist element in the most self-proclaimed materialist texts. He thus took a tremendously liberating step, opening up the entire field of philosophy to Marxism.

"Philosophy and the Spontaneous Philosophy of the Scientists" and Other Essays (1967)

The title essay, "Philosophy and the Spontaneous Philosophy of the Scientists" was published as a book in Althusser's series with Maspero in 1974. It consists of a series of lectures Althusser delivered in the Fall of 1967 on the relation between philosophy and science, or rather between philosophical and scientific practice. The role of philosophy appeared to be very limited: it did not state the truth, it did not even refer to a reality outside of itself. Instead philosophy remained within itself, working on itself by drawing lines of demarcation. This activity does not doom philosophy to self-referential irrelevance, however; because scientific practice remains inescapably enveloped in philosophy (the spontaneous philosophy of scientists), the lines of demarcation it draws separate science from ideology. This extraordinary text has not received the attention it deserves.

The Future Lasts Forever (1992)

Althusser's autobiography adds little if anything to our knowledge of his philosophical and political writings, except perhaps the fantasies that accompanied or were retroactively projected upon them. It provides a demonstrably false account both of Althusser's knowledge and interests, as well as the political and theoretical relations which he maintained and in which he flourished throughout much of the 1960s. One might profitably compare the Althusser constructed here with our sense of the writer of Althusser's *Lettres à Franca,* the bulk of which were written between 1961 and 1966. Some commentators have ceded to the temptation to declare the narrator of the *Future* the "real" Althusser in contrast to the persona projected in the philosophical and political writings. As I have suggested in Chapter 3, such an assertion fails to acknowledge the fundamental absence of Althusser from his own self-portrait.

The Spectre of Hegel

This collection consists of Althusser's early writings, or Althusser before Althusser, as his editor puts it. Most notably, the book contains the entire text of his Master's thesis, "On Content in the Thought of G. W. F. Hegel," a comprehensive work that exhibits a sympathy with Hegel and suggests that Hegelianism was Althusser's conduit out of the Catholicism of his youth. Two other particularly interesting essays are his very critical reviews of the two most important figures in French mid-century Hegel studies, Alexandre Kojève and Jean Hyppolite, in which he charges them with abstracting from Hegel a stage in the process of Spirit becoming itself, and making it into a human essence.

Writings on Psychoanalysis

This is an extremely valuable collection of some of Althusser's most important essays. It replicates the French version, with one regrettable omission, "Trois notes sur le discours," a draft that marks the first version of the notion of the interpellated subject. It not only contains the great essay "Freud and Lacan" from 1964, but contains the documents of what Althusser's editors call the "Tbilisi Affair." Althusser had been invited to present a paper at an international symposium on the unconscious in Soviet Georgia in October 1976. He hastily wrote a draft, published here as "The Discovery of Dr. Freud." He sent this to a number of friends including Elisabeth Roudinesco, Michel Pecheux and Jacques Nassif. All expressed dismay not only about its sloppiness, but about its rather straightforward critique of Lacan as having degenerated into formalism. He wrote another essay ("On Marx and Freud") which, while interesting in certain respects, sidestepped the Lacan question. "Dr Freud's Discovery" was later published without Althusser's consent. The entire dossier of the controversy, including a letter from Roudinesco, is included here. Also included are long letters on psychoanalytic theory that Althusser wrote to his (very non-Lacanian) analyst, René Diatkine, as well as to Lacan himself.

Écrits philosophiques et politiques, vols I–II (1994)

The two volumes represent a selection of materials from the large archive of Althusser's manuscripts, notes and letters for posthumous publication. Both volumes were scrupulously edited and prepared by François Matheron and include all the variants of texts of which different versions exist. Volume I consists of the material translated into English in *The Spectre of Hegel*, together with a substantial text from 1978, "Marx dans ses limites," or "Marx within his limits," which explores what Althusser argues is a political and theoretical crisis of Marxism. In addition, volume I also includes two post-1980 pieces, one of which, the fragment entitled, "Le courant souterrain du matérialisme du rencontre" or "The Subterranean Current of the Materialism of the Encounter," defines what Althusser calls an "aleatory materialism." According to this conception, what we call historical necessity is itself a product of chance encounters, which always occur in the void, without foundation or origin. He calls a somewhat strange array of witnesses to testify on his behalf: Lucretius, Machiavelli and Spinoza, together with Hobbes, Rousseau and Heidegger. The idea of a materialism of the encounter is not a new one for Althusser, the concept can be found in his work as early as the mid-1960s, but the highly speculative readings of Hobbes and Heidegger, together with the notion of a philosophy of nothingness, mark a shift in his thinking. Volume II contains the text of the book *Machiavelli and Us*, and the essays on art found in *Lenin and Philosophy*. It also contains a number of interesting critiques of structuralism, phenomenology and humanism. The second volume also includes an interesting sketch of the "philosophical conjuncture" of mid-sixties France as Althusser saw it. Most of these pieces will be published in translation by Verso over the next few years.

Sur la reproduction (1995)

This text, originally entitled *De la superstructure*, constitutes the work from which the ISAs (Ideological State Apparatuses) essay was extracted. It is a strange, composite text, part political and philosophical manual and part intervention in the debates on the French Left following the revolt of 1968. It is written in a quasi-popular style, unlike most of Althusser's works. It is of interest primarily as it helps us construct a genealogy of some of the key concepts in the 1970 ideology essay. Althusser spends considerable time discussing the function of law in capitalist societies and his discussion merits commentary. Further, a comparison between the published ISAs essay and the corresponding sections of *Sur la reproduction* show that Althusser systematically removed all references to the ideological apparatuses as sites of struggle rather than machines for the reproduction of the relations of production and exploitation. He thus chose to present a functionalist theory of ideology for tactical reasons, demonstrating the difficulty of revolution in the face of the materiality of ideology.

Lettres à Franca, 1961–1973 (1998)

This large volume (800 pages) contains the letters that Althusser wrote to Franca Madonia, the Italian translator of Claude Lévi-Strauss, Gerard Genette and the poet Jacques Prévert, together with a much smaller number of letters by Madonia herself. Most of the letters were written during the period between 1961 and 1965, Althusser's most creative period, and Madonia was an individual of extraordinary political and cultural sophistication who served as one of Althusser's interlocutors. While it might be regretted that the editors chose to include letters of a purely personal nature that express nothing other than the state of the relationship, at least half the letters contain Althusser's reflections on his work and the work of some of France's most celebrated thinkers. The correspondence contains interesting remarks, sometimes extended, on such figures as Barthes, Foucault, Derrida, Lévi-Strauss, and Lacan. Althusser also reflects on Marx, Freud, Spinoza, Machiavelli and Hegel, among others. The reader will see from the inside the exhilaration of philosophical and theoretical discovery and Althusser's vivid interest in art, literature and cinema.

Sur la philosophie (1994)

This text contains an extended interview with Althusser by the Mexican philosopher Fernanda Navarro in the mid-1980s, which was published in Spanish translation in 1988. It was here that Althusser made public his conception of an aleatory materialism. Interestingly, he did not present it so much as a change in his thinking, but rather as the trajectory of his thought from the outset, an element that he chose not to make explicit until the end of his philosophical and political career. Here he discusses Epicurus and Lucretius (whose work he read closely, as his notes in the archive demonstrate), Heidegger, and Wittgenstein, philosophers whose work is not usually associated with Althusser. There is also a fascinating but extremely elliptical comment on Derrida's notion of the trace.

Solitude de Machiavel, ed. Yves Sintomer (1998)

While many of the essays collected here (e.g., "Lenin and Philosophy" and "Elements of Self-Criticism") are available in English editions, other valuable texts are included. "Sur l'objectivité de l'histoire" is a critical response to the French phenomenological tradition from the mid-1950s. Althusser's review of Raymond Polin's *La Politique morale de John Locke* presents a fairly original and provocative reading of Locke's major works. The volume also includes the transcription of the lively discussion that followed Althusser's presentation of "Lenin and Philosophy" at the Société Française de Philosophie in 1968. There is a particularly interesting exchange between him and Paul Ricoeur, as well as commentary by Stanislaus Breton, a Jesuit who later became very close to Althusser.

Major Works on Althusser

Note The reader will note the omission here of works discussed in the Introduction, namely those works that defined the debates about Althusser in the 1970s and early 1980s. My intention here is to indicate the resources for a genuine reading of Althusser beyond imitation (which inevitably and usually unconsciously differs from what it imitates) or rejection. Those who are interested in reconstructing the Anglo-American reception of Althusser (which has an interest apart from whatever interpretation its authors offer of Althusser) must of course consult Thompson, Hindess and Hirst, Eagleton and Ted Benton, among others. I firmly maintain, however, that the studies discussed below are to a great extent unencumbered by the political and philosophical imperatives of the earlier period and will therefore prove more helpful to those who wish to understand before they judge Althusser.

Gregory Elliot, *Althusser: The Detour of Theory* (1987):

Easily the most authoritative and comprehensive account of the work published during Althusser's lifetime. Elliot's meticulous reading of Althusser's key pre-1980 texts not only traces the detours of Althusser's long theoretical journey, but places these texts in the political conjuncture that overdetermined them and outside of which they can't be understood. He reconstructs the debates within the international Communist movement and within the French party in particular and demonstrates their relevance even to Althusser's most "philosophical" works. Elliot's text demonstrated the irrelevance of most of the critiques of and debates about Althusser and in this sense recast the entire discussion, allowing new ideas and readings to emerge.

Yann Moulier Boutang, *Louis Althusser: une biographie, 1918–1956* (1992)

This is the first half of a comprehensive biography of Althusser based on massive research; the author has not only mastered the archival materials (including Althusser's correspondence), he conducted hundreds of interviews with those who knew Althusser at various stages in his life. The author not only describes Althusser's familial and cultural background, but also the experiences that shaped the first half of his life, his life before his major works. Moulier describes in detail Althusser's experience at the Lycée, his encounter with two important Catholic philosophers, Jean Guitton and Jean Lacroix, and his subsequent attraction to right-wing Catholic and Monarchist movements. He also demonstrates the importance of his experience as a prisoner-of-war for his subsequent development as a Communist intellectual. Moulier provides a valuable sketch of the post-war French Left and Althusser's evolution within it, especially in the peculiar context of the École Normale Supérieure, a context often impenetrable to outsiders. The biography dispels many of the myths about Althusser, including the most damning of all, those invented by the philosopher himself.

E. Ann Kaplan and Michael Sprinker (eds), *The Althusserian Legacy* (1993)

This is a collection of papers presented at a conference on Althusser held at the State University of New York, Stony Brook, in 1988 in which the diverse strands of "Althusserianism" and even certain anti-Althusserianisms came together and a new wave of scholarly work on Althusser was born. Balibar's essay marks an attempt to understand the "non-contemporaneity" of Althusser's work after 1980. This theme also occupies Gregory Elliot's examination of Althusser's solitude. Peter Schottler, a former student of Althusser's, discusses the relation of Althusser's conception of historical time to that of the Annales school of historiography. Warren Montag attempts to connect Althusser's treatment of reading to that of Spinoza. Stephen Resnick and Richard Wolff describe the vision of Althusser that shaped the project of *Rethinking Marxism.* Both Alex Callinicos and Michele Barrett, who were once identified with Althusser in some way, offer severe criticisms of his work. Appended to the collection is an interview with Jacques Derrida conducted by Michael Sprinker. It is extremely interesting, even if many of Derrida's assertions about the extent and limitations of Althusser's philosophical knowledge (as well as the lack of philosophical discussion between the two men) are not substantiated by the evidence contained in the archive.

Gregory Elliot (ed.), *Althusser: A Critical Reader* (1994)

While this text contains some earlier texts on Althusser, Hobsbawm's surprisingly appreciative piece and historian Pierre Vilar's interrogation of Althusser's view of history, and Ricoeur's critique of Althusser's conception of ideology, there are also some important new viewpoints. David Macey describes the complex relation between Althusser and Lacan, although without reference to the post-1990 publications. Francis Mulhern provides an excellent overview of Althusser's effects in the realm of literary theory.

Depositions: Althusser, Balibar, Macherey and the Labor of Reading, Yale French Studies 88 (1995)

This issue of Yale French Studies, edited by Jacques Lezra, contains a number of extremely interesting and valuable essays, including those by Balibar and Macherey. Balibar's essay presents an overview of the main themes of his own work up to 1990. Macherey discusses the notion of subjectivity in Foucault's reading of Raymond Roussel. In addition, the volume features essays on Althusser from very diverse points of view: Judith Butler critically examines the ISAs essay, specifically interrogating the notion of interpellation. Ellen Rooney takes as her object the notion of reading in Althusser. Jacques Lezra discusses the concept of theoretical labor, the activity of theory itself. Warren Montag reads the ISAs essay and Foucault's *Discipline and Punish* as together constituting an extended dialogue on the place of the body in the system of subjection. Michael Sprinker provides an excellent overview of Althusser's theoretical legacy.

Antonio Callari and David F. Ruccio (eds), *Postmodern Materialism and the Future of Marxist Theory: Essays in the Althusserian Tradition* (1996)

This collection contains some of the most interesting work on Althusser in the last decade. The editors, Antonio Callari and David Ruccio, are founders of the journal *Rethinking Marxism*, a journal that has played a crucial role in rehabilitating Althusser's reputation and in publishing work that is either a commentary on or inspired by Althusser. Represented here is the work of a number of economists associated with the journal: Richard Wolff, Stephen Cullenberg, Bruce Roberts, J. K. Gibson-Graham, and others. The essays by Balibar (on the idea of structural causality) and Emmanuel Terray (on Althusser and Machiavelli) are particularly interesting in that these former colleagues of Althusser reflect on his work in a way that neither condemns it nor affirms it as it is. Rather, they both call attention to its impasses, as well as to the overlooked and undeveloped strains in it. Antonio Negri's essay is a fascinating reading of Althusser's post-1980 work. Warren Montag discusses the relation of the idea of interpellation to Althusser's analyses of Hobbes and Locke. Gregory Elliot provides an extremely valuable overview of Althusser's life and work

Rereading Althusser, Rethinking Marxism, 10:3 (1998)

This special issue of *Rethinking Marxism* is of particular interest in that it represents the new wave of Althusser scholarship to emerge internationally in the 1990s. A number of the essays examine the publications of the 1990s. Francois Matheron, who edited the posthumous publications and who organized the Althusser Archive, furnishes an extremely rigorous account of the recurrence of the notion of *le vide* or "the void" in Althusser's work. Gregory Elliot examines the notion of the aleatory in Althusser's later work. Ted Stolze, using unpublished materials, discusses a philosophical correspondence between Althusser and Deleuze concerning structuralism. Max Statkiewicz's essay on Althusser's unfinished piece on Brecht and Marx will be of particular interest to students of literature. Warren Montag discusses the tension between structure and singularity throughout Althusser's work.

Sylvain Lazarus (ed.), *Politique et philosophie dans l'oeuvre de Louis Althusser* (1993)

This collection brings together a number of Althusser's former students and colleagues, some of whom, such as Jacques Rancière and Alain Badiou, broke with Althusser in the 1960s for both political and philosophical reasons. Badiou's remarks on Althusser's conception of philosophy are particularly relevant. There is an interesting discussion of Althusser's conception of law by Francine Demichel. François Regnault, a former student, provides a moving overview of

Althusser's work. Balibar and Terray also contribute essays which have since appeared in English translation.

Pierre Raymond (ed.), *Althusser philosophe* (1997)

Raymond, another former student of Althusser's, has collected essays on Althusser's reading of philosophers, especially Spinoza, Montesquieu, Hegel and Marx. Pierre-François Moreau, one of the world's most eminent Spinoza scholars, compares Althusser's conception of philosophy to that of Spinoza and gives a fascinating account of Althusser's appropriation of his favorite thinker. Stanislaus Breton's essay on Althusser and religion examines Althusser's work from beginning to end, from his early Catholicism to his interest in liberation theology.

Other relevant materials

Pierre Macherey, *A Theory of Literary Production* (1966)

This important work decisively influenced both Marxist and non-Marxist approaches to literature. Written as part of a collective project involving Althusser and others, such as Alain Badiou, Etienne Balibar and Michel Pecheux, Macherey's text marked the most pointed critique of structuralism from the Althusserian camp. It is an elliptical and dense work, embodying the passion of discovery. Macherey identifies and dismantles the theoretical obstacles to barring the way to a knowledge of literary texts in their objective existence and then proceeds to analyze the work of Jules Verne (a "minor" author). It is left to the reader to develop a theory adequate to an analysis of literary and cultural artifacts.

Pierre Macherey, *The Object of Literature* (1990)

The French title, *A quoi pense la littérature?* ("What does literature think about"), better indicates the objective of the work. In an important sense, this text neither repeats nor repudiates the earlier work. Instead, Macherey explores what was left largely unspecified in *A Theory*, namely the raw material out of which literature is fashioned.

He advances the idea that literature (which emerges in its specificity only in the eighteenth century) maintains a privileged relation to philosophy, not because philosophy is the truth of literature, but because they are both shaped out of the same material and can't finally be separated. Literature, argues Macherey, performs philosophical concepts and thus exposes a dimension that escapes the comprehension of philosophy. Both literature and philosophy elude themselves and can be grasped only in the mirror of the other, a mirror that reflects those contradictions that make them what they are.

Pierre Macherey, *In a Materialist Way* (1998)

This work is a collection of essays from the 1980s and 1990s (the exception is Macherey's first published article, with an introduction by Althusser). Many of the essays are commentaries on Macherey's contemporaries such as Lacan, Foucault and Deleuze. A section is devoted to Macherey's work on Spinoza. In addition, there is an interesting piece provocatively entitled "For a Theory of Literary Reproduction," in which Macherey argues that a work is irreducible to the causes of its production and that it is constantly remade and rewritten in interaction with other works and in new historical situations.

Warren Montag and Ted Stolze (eds), *The New Spinoza* (1997)

This collection of essays documents the importance of Spinoza for postwar French philosophy in general and Althusser in particular. It includes an extremely interesting and accessible essay on Spinoza that Althusser originally wrote as part of his autobiography. Most of the other contributors were once his students: Balibar, Macherey, André Tosel, Pierre-François Moreau. Also included are essays by Deleuze, Antonio Negri, Gabriel Albiac and Alexandre Matheron. All the themes of Althusser's work are to be found in these reflections on Spinoza, whose texts are unavoidable for anyone who would study Althusser seriously.

Michel Pecheux, *Language, Semantics and Ideology* (1976)

Pecheux's work marks perhaps the major attempt to extend

Althusser's conception of ideology as explored in the ISAs essay. It grows out of the discussion between Althusser and his students in 1966–7 on the relation of discourse to ideology and on the interpellation, a discussion in which the developing work of Lacan figured heavily. Pecheux, a linguist, considers at length Althusser's proposition that ideology and the unconscious (although the unconscious understood by Lacan rather than Freud) are linked. It is a work that deserves more scrutiny that it has received.

References

Albiac, G. et al. (1997) *Lire Althusser Aujourd 'hui.* Paris: L'Harmatton.

Albiac, Gabriel (1998) "Althusser, Reader of Althusser: Autobiography as Fictional Genre." *Rethinking Marxism* 3 (1998): 80–9.

Althusser, Louis (1964) "Conferenza dibatto del Professore Louis Althusser." *La Provincia di Forti,* January 8, 1964, pp. 5–10.

Althusser, Louis (1969) *For Marx.* London: Verso.

Althusser, Louis (1971) *Lenin and Philosophy, and Other Essays.* New York: Monthly Review Press.

Althusser, Louis (1972) *Politics and History,* trans. Ben Brewster. Paris: New Left Books.

Althusser, Louis (1973) *Essays in Self-Criticism,* trans. Grahame Lock. Norfolk: New Left Books.

Althusser, Louis (1975) *Reading Capital,* trans. Ben Brewster. London: New Left Books.

Althusser, Louis (1992) *The Future Lasts Forever.* New York: New York University Press.

Althusser, Louis (1994) *Sur la philosophie.* Paris: Gallimard.

Althusser, Louis (1994a) *Écrits philosophiques et politiques,* vol. 1. Paris: Stock/IMEC.

Althusser, Louis (1994b) *Écrits philosophiques et politiques,* vol. 2. Paris: Stock/IMEC.

Althusser, Louis (1995) *Sur la reproduction.* Paris: Presses Universitaires de France.

Althusser, Louis (1996a) *Lire le Capital.* Paris: Presses Universitaires de France.

Althusser, Louis (1996b) *Pour Marx.* Paris: La Découverte.

Althusser, Louis (1997a) "Part I: Spinoza." *The New Spinoza,* eds. Warren Montag and Ted Stolze. Minneapolis: University of Minnesota Press, pp. 3–20.

Althusser, Louis (1997b) *The Spectre of Hegel: Early Writings,* trans. G. M. Goshgarian. London: Verso.

Althusser, Louis (1998) *Lettres à Franca, 1961–1973.* Paris: Stock/IMEC.

Althusser, Louis (1999) *Writings on Psychoanalysis.* New York: Columbia University Press.

Anderson, Perry (1976) *Considerations on Western Marxism.* London: New Left Books.

Anderson, Perry (1983) *In the Tracks of Historical Materialism.* London: Verso.

Badiou, Alain (1993) "Qu'est-ce que Louis Althusser entend par 'philosophie'." *Politique et philosophie dans l'oeuvre de Louis Althusser,* ed. Sylvain Lazarus. Paris: Presses Universitaires de France, pp. 29–46.

Balibar, Étienne (1993a) "The Non-Contemporaneity of Althusser." *The Althusserian Legacy,* ed. E. Ann Kaplan and Michael Sprinker. London: Verso, pp. 1–16.

Balibar, Étienne (1993b) "L'Objet d'Althusser." *Politique et philosophie dans l'oeuvre de Louis Althusser,* ed. Sylvain Lazarus. Paris: Presses Universitaires de France.

Balibar, Étienne (1996) "Structural Causality, Overdetermination, and Antagonism." *Postmodern Materialism and the Future of Marxist Theory,* ed. Antonio Callari and David F. Ruccio. Hanover: Wesleyan University Press, pp. 109–19.

Balibar, Étienne (1995) *The Philosophy of Marx,* trans. Chris Turner. London: Verso.

Beattie, James (1783) *Dissertations Moral and Critical.* London.

Beckett, Samuel (1954) *Waiting for Godot.* New York: Grove Press.

Beckett, Samuel (1976) *Three Novels: Molloy, Malone Dies, The Unnameable.* New York: Grove Press.

Benton, Ted (1984) *The Rise and Fall of Structural Marxism: Althusser and his Influence.* London: Macmillan.

Bloom, Harold (1994) *The Western Canon.* New York: Harcourt Brace.

Braunthal, Julius (1966) *History of the International: 1864–1914,* trans. Henry Collins and Kenneth Mitchell. London: Thomas Nelson and Sons.

Callari, Antonio and Ruccio, David (eds.) (1996) *Postmodern Materialism and the Future of Marxist Theory: Essays in the Althusserian Tradition.* Hanover: Weslyan University Press.

Callinicos, Alex (1993) "What is Living and What is Dead in the Philosophy of Althusser." *The Althusserian Legacy,* ed. E. Ann Kaplan and Michael Sprinker. London: Verso, pp. 39–50.

Conrad, Joseph (1962) *"Heart of Darkness" and "The Secret Sharer".* New York: Signet.

Conrad, Joseph (1975) *The Nigger of the "Narcissus", Typhoon and other Stories.* Harmondsworth: Penguin Books.

Conrad, Joseph (1983) *Heart of Darkness.* Harmondsworth: Penguin Books.

Cullenberg, Stephen (1996) "Althusser and the Decentering of the Marxist Totality." *Postmodern Materialism and the Future of Marxist Theory,* ed. Antonio Callari and David F. Ruccio. Hanover: Wesleyan University Press, pp. 120–49.

Defoe, Daniel (1965) *Robinson Crusoe.* Harmondsworth: Penguin Books.

Deleuze, Gilles and Felix Guattari (1999) *Anti-Oedipus: Introduction to Schizoanalysis.* London: Routledge.

Eagleton, Terry (1976) *Criticism and Ideology: A Study in Marxist Literary Theory.* London: New Left Books.

Eagleton, Terry (1986) *Against the Grain: Essays, 1975–1985.* London: Verso.

Elliot, Gregory (1987) *Althusser: The Detour of Theory.* London: Verso.

Elliot, Gregory (1993) "Althusser's Solitude." *The Althusserian Legacy,* ed. E. Ann Kaplan and Michael Sprinker. London: Verso, pp. 17–38.

Elliot, Gregory (1994) *Althusser: A Critical Reader.* Cambridge: Blackwell.

Elliot, Gregory (1996) "Analysis Terminated, Analysis Interminable." *Postmodern*

Materialism and the Future of Marxist Theory, ed. Antonio Callari and David F. Ruccio. Hanover: Wesleyan University Press, pp. 337–56.

Elliot, Gregory (1998) "The Necessity of Contingency: Some Notes." *Rethinking Marxism* 3: 74–9.

Elster, Jon (1985) *Making Sense of Marx*. New York: Cambridge University Press.

Foucault, Michel (1978) *The History of Sexuality*. New York: Pantheon.

Foucault, Michel (1994) *Dits et Écrits 1954–1988*, ed. Daniel Defert and François Edwald. Paris: Éditions Gallimard.

Foucault, Michel (1995) *Discipline and Punish*, trans. Alan Sheridan. New York: Vintage Books.

Gallagher, Catherine (1989) "Marxism and the New Historian." *The New Historicism*, ed. H. Aram Veeser. New York: Routledge, Chapman and Hall.

Habermas, Jürgen (1987) *The Philosophical Discourse of Modernity: Twelve Lectures*, trans. Fredrick Lawrence. Cambridge, Mass.: MIT Press.

Hindess, Barry and Hirst, Paul (1977) *Mode of Production and Social Formation*. London: Macmillan.

Hochschild, Adam (1998) *King Leopold's Ghost*. Boston: Houghton Mifflin.

Howlett, Marc-Vincent (1997) "Le Théâtre n'est-il pour Althusser qu'un 'Risque Fictif'." *Lire Althusser Aujourd 'hui*, ed. G. Albiac et al. Paris: L'Harmatton, pp. 115–38.

Jameson, Fredric (1981) *The Political Unconscious: Narrative as a Socially Symbolic Act*. Ithaca, NY: Cornell University Press.

Jameson, Fredric (1984) "Postmodernism or the Cultural Logic of Late Capitalism." *New Left Review I* 146: 53–92.

Jameson, Fredric (1989) "Marxism and Postmodernism." *New Left Review I* 176: 31–45.

Kaplan, E. Ann and Michael Sprinker (ed.) (1993) *The Althusserian Legacy*. London: Verso.

Lacan Jacques (1977) *Écrits*, trans. Alan Sheridan. New York: Norton.

Lazarus, Sylvain (ed.) (1993) *Politique et philosophie dans l'oeuvre de Louis Althusser*. Paris: Presses Universitaires de France.

Lock, Grahame (1996) "Subject, Interpellation, and Ideology." *Postmodern Materialism and the Future of Marxist Theory*, ed. Antonio Callari and David F. Ruccio. Hanover: Wesleyan University Press, pp. 69–90.

Locke, John (1980) *The Second Treatise of Government*. Indianapolis: Hackett.

Macherey, Pierre (1978) *Towards a Theory of Literary Production*, trans. Geoffrey Wall. Boston: Routledge and Kegan Paul.

Macherey, Pierre (1999) *Histoire de dinosaure*. Paris: Presses Universitaires de France.

Macherey, Pierre (1998) *In a Materialist Way*, ed. Warren Montag. London: Verso.

Macherey, Pierre (1995) *The Object of Literature*. Cambridge: Cambridge University Press.

Macherey, Pierre (1982) "Interview: Étienne Balibar & Pierre Machery." *Diacritics* 12: 46–52.

Marx, Karl (1998) *The German Ideology*. New York: Prometheus.

Matheron, François (1998) "The Recurrence of the Void in Louis Althusser." *Rethinking Marxism* 3: 22–37.

Mocnik, Ratsko (1993) "Ideology and Fantasy." *The Althusserian Legacy*, ed. E. Ann Kaplan and Michael Sprinker. London: Verso, pp. 139–56.

Montag, Warren (1993) "Spinoza and Althusser Against Hermeneutics: Interpretation or Intervention?" *The Althusserian Legacy*, ed. E. Ann Kaplan and Michael Sprinker. London: Verso, pp. 51–8.

Montag, Warren (1996) "Beyond Force and Consent: Althusser, Spinoza, Hobbes." *Postmodern Materialism and the Future of Marxist Theory*, ed. Antonio Callari and David F. Ruccio. Hanover: Wesleyan University Press, pp. 91–108.

Montag, Warren (1998) "Althusser's Nominalism: Structure and Singularity (1962–6)." *Rethinking Marxism* 3: 64–73.

Montag, Warren and Ted Stolze (ed.) (1987) *The New Spinoza*. Minneapolis: University of Minneapolis Press.

Negri, Antonio (1997) "Machiavel selon Althusser." *Lire Althusser Aujourd'hui*, ed. G. Albiac et al. Paris: L'Harmatton, pp. 139–58.

Negri, Antonio (1996) "Notes on the Evolution of the Thought of the Later Althusser." *Postmodern Materialism and the Future of Marxist Theory*, ed. Antonio Callari and David F. Ruccio. Hanover: Wesleyan University Press, pp. 51–68.

Pecheux, Michel (1975) *Language, Semantics and Ideology*. New York: St Martin's Press.

Ponomarev, B. N. (1986) *The International Working Class Movement: Problems of History and Theory*, vol. 2. Moscow: Progress Publishers.

Raymond, Pierre (ed.) (1997) *Althusser philosophe*. Paris: Presses Universitaires de France.

Resnick, Stephen and Richard Wolff (1993) "Althusser's Liberation of Marxian Theory." *The Althusserian Legacy*, ed. E. Ann Kaplan and Michael Sprinker. London: Verso, pp. 59–72.

Sokal, Alan D. and J. Bricmont (1999) *Fashionable Nonsense: Postmodern Intellectuals' Abuse of Science*. New York: Picador.

Spinoza, Baruch (1991) *Tractatus Theologico-Politicus*, trans. Samuel Shirley. New York: Brill Academic Publishers.

Spinoza, Baruch (1992) *Ethics*, trans. Samuel Shirley. Indianapolis: Hacket Publishing.

Sprinker, Michael (1987) *Imaginary Relations*. New York: Verso.

Statkiewicz, Max (1998) "Theater and/or Ideology: The Notion of *Spostamento* in Althusser's Theory of Theatrical Praxis." *Rethinking Marxism* 3: 38–50.

Stolze, Ted (1998) "Deleuze and Althusser: Flirting with Structuralism." *Rethinking Marxism* 3: 51–63.

Terry, Emmanuel (1993) "Une Recontre: Althusser et Machiavel." Politique et philosophie dans l'Oeuvre de Louis Althusser, ed. Sylvain Lazarus. Paris: Presses Universitaires de France, pp. 137–60.

Terry, Emmanuel (1996) "An Encounter: Althusser and Machiavelli." *Postmodern*

Materialism and the Future of Marxist Theory, ed. Antonio Callari and David F. Ruccio. Hanover: Wesleyan University Press, pp. 257–77.

Thompson, E. P. (1995) *The Poverty of Theory, or An Orrery of Errors.* London: Merlin Press.

Vandervort, Bruce (1998) *Wars of Imperial Conquest in Africa, 1830–1914.* Bloomington: Indiana University Press.

Wolff, Richard (1996) "Althusser and Hegel: Making Marxist Explanations Anti-essentialist and Dialectical." *Postmodern Materialism and the Future of Marxist Theory*, ed. Antonio Callari and David F. Ruccio. Hanover: Wesleyan University Press, pp. 150–66.

Wolff, Richard (1998) "A Note on Althusser's Importance for Marxism Today." *Rethinking Marxism* 3: 90–2.

Index